D0527398

The Sarkozy Phenomenon

Nick Hewlett

SOCIETAS

essays in political
& cultural criticism

imprint-academic.com

Copyright © Nick Hewlett, 2011

The moral rights of the author have been asserted.
No part of this publication may be reproduced in any form
without permission, except for the quotation of brief passages
in criticism and discussion.

Published in the UK by Societas
Imprint Academic, PO Box 200, Exeter EX5 5YX, UK

Published in the USA by Societas
Imprint Academic, Philosophy Documentation Center
PO Box 7147, Charlottesville, VA 22906-7147, USA

ISBN 9781845402396

A CIP catalogue record for this book is available from the
British Library and US Library of Congress

Other books by Nick Hewlett

Badiou, Balibar, Rancière. Re-thinking Emancipation,
Continuum, 2007.

Democracy in Modern France, Continuum, 2003.

Modern French Politics. Conflict and Consensus since 1945,
Polity, 1998.

Contents

Acknowledgements

I would like to thank James Shields, David Lees and two anonymous readers for comments either on draft chapters of this book or on papers which influenced it. In particular, I wish to thank Emmanuel Godin for his careful and insightful reading of the whole draft manuscript and for his very helpful comments on it. The final version is, of course, my responsibility alone. (Translations from the French, unless otherwise indicated, are also my own.) I am also grateful to Anthony Freeman at Imprint Academic for his enthusiasm for the book from the start, to Rosalind Davies for her copy editing and to Jacqueline Speel for meticulous indexing. Earlier versions of parts of Chapter Two appeared in a book edited by Tony Chafer and Emmanuel Godin, entitled *The End of the French Exception?* (Palgrave, 2010) and in *Modern and Contemporary France* (XV: 4, Nov. 2007).

Thanks also to Gary Browning, for many conversations about many things, to my children Emily and Gus, who have many thought-provoking ideas of their own, and to Bridget Taylor for putting up with constant reports on the day-to-day progress of my work.

This book is dedicated to my friends in France, whose generosity and friendship over many years have been important for me personally and also valuable in enabling a better understanding of France and French politics.

Nick Hewlett
January 2011

Abbreviations

CFE-CGC	Confédération française de l'encadrement-Confédération générale des cadres
CFTC	Confédération française des travailleurs chrétiens
CFDT	Confédération française démocratique du travail
CGT	Confédération générale du travail
CGT-FO	Confédération générale du travail-Force ouvrière
CPE	Contrat première embauche
EDF	Electricité de France
ENA	Ecole nationale d'administration
FN	Front national
FO	Force ouvrière
GDF	Gaz de France
MEDEF	Mouvement des entreprises de France
MODEM	Mouvement démocrate
NPNS	Ni putes, ni soumises
OECD	Organisation for Economic Cooperation and Development
ORTF	Office de la radiodiffusion-télévision française
PCF	Parti communiste français
PS	Parti socialiste

RATP	Régie autonome des transports parisiens
RPF	Rassemblement du peuple français
RMI	Revenu minimum d'insertion
RSA	Revenu de solidarité active
SMIC	Salaire minimum interprofessionnel de croissance
SNCF	Société nationale des chemins de fer
SPD	Sozialdemokratische partei Deutschlands
SUD	Solidaires, unitaires et démocratiques
TEPA	Loi en faveur du travail, de l'emploi et du pouvoir d'achat
UDF	Union pour la démocratie française
UMP	Union pour un mouvement populaire (April–October 2002, Union pour une majorité présidentielle)
UNSA	Union nationale des syndicats autonomes

Pour mes amis en France

Chapter One

Introduction

I'll be a president like Louis de Funès in *Le Grand Restaurant*: servile with the powerful, insufferable with the weak. I love it.

Nicolas Sarkozy, 16 February 2007
(quoted in Jeudy and Vigogne, 2007: 152)

From time to time, in one country or another, national political leaders emerge who offer themselves as vehicles for profound transformation, making it clear that they wish to change significantly the direction in which their country is travelling. In order for such individuals to achieve high office and to have a significant influence on the course of the political, social and economic life of a country, personal characteristics are of course important; in addition to being hungry for power, they are often hard-working, have well-honed oratory skills and charm. But personal characteristics alone are never sufficient for the success of such individuals. The circumstances in which they are operating must also be favourable to their project and, crucially, the leader must have the support of powerful groups both in politics and in the rest of society as well. Just as importantly, other groups who oppose the leader must be in sufficient disarray that they are unable to garner enough support to prevent the leader and their supporters from achieving substantial power and carrying out their wishes. The modern governmental history of France is peppered with heads of state whose rule may aptly be described as personalised, authoritarian and populist. The latest such example, Nicolas Sarkozy, has thus been likened to Charles de Gaulle, Philippe Pétain, Napoleon III and Napoleon I.

When Nicolas Sarkozy was elected president of the republic on 6 May 2007 France entered a decidedly new phase in national politics. We saw the victory of a candidate with the image of a tough, innovative leader apparently prepared to say the previously unsayable and to embrace drastic measures with open arms where this was deemed necessary for the good of the nation. He had made it clear from the start of his campaign that he did not wish to be seen as a mere representative of the centre-right, which three previous presidents after de Gaulle, arguably, had been. These were Georges Pompidou (from 1969 to 1974), Valéry Giscard d'Estaing (1974–81) and Jacques Chirac (1995–2007). Rather, Sarkozy placed great emphasis on himself as a special individual who had a mission to break with the past and do something decidedly different. Thus, despite having held three key ministerial positions under President Chirac and despite having had a substantial influence on important aspects of the Chirac presidency, one of his most-used campaigning words in 2007 was the French *rupture*. France needed to break, he argued, with years of economic stagnation, social strife and a lacklustre image on the international stage. The country needed to be jolted into a process of modernisation and he was elected with a mandate to make profound changes, as someone who, as he says at the very beginning of his autobiography, wants to be seen as a man who gets things done: 'I've always wanted to take action' (Sarkozy 2006: 1).

Certainly, it was clear that Sarkozy sought to be identified with a tough, law and order agenda, and during his two stints as Minister of the Interior under President Chirac he had already established a track record as precisely this. It was also evident that he wished to steer France in a more market-oriented direction than had been the case previously. This conformed with his position as a right-wing leader of the early twenty-first century in one of the most economically successful nations on earth by conventional criteria (although it is often not conceived as such). But Sarkozy was also a maverick and was not content with limiting himself to a mainstream right-wing policy agenda and there were also frequent references to left-oriented sources of inspiration, such as the Socialist leaders Léon Blum and Jean Jaurès and the communist resister Guy Môquet, who was executed by the Nazis in Châteaubriant in October 1941 at the age of seventeen. Moreover, Sarkozy's election manifesto and campaign speeches time and again emphasised the importance of rewarding hard work on the part of ordinary people and promised to raise standards of living for all. Nevertheless, precisely what Sarkozy planned to do once in office was not clear, as both his campaign and manifesto were an idiosyncratic mix of determined statements of intent which, when all these statements were put together, lacked coherence and certainly did not amount to a strategy. It was clear both from the election campaign and from the immediate aftermath of the election that what Sarkozy wanted most was a personal mandate which would give him a degree of personal power that had not been seen since de Gaulle, who was president of the republic from 1958 to 1969. It was also clear that he would use this power to attempt to achieve far-reaching neo-liberal reform of the economy and a greater emphasis on law and order than had been seen for many years.

Sarkozy's actual presidency has been no less extraordinary. His style and practice is indeed deeply autocratic and in his actions and words he wishes to make it clear that he and he alone holds supreme political authority. He seeks personal involvement in as many areas of policy-making as possible, often eclipsing the functions of the prime minister, whose own role in government has become less significant than it has been for many years. The president controls tightly what ministers do and say and demands absolute loyalty. Close advisors such as Claude Guéant and Henri Gaino are a dominant force and carefully control the image of Sarkozy and his regime as conveyed to the media and thus to the country as a whole. As soon as he became president — or *hyperprésident* as he was soon dubbed — he set about reforming in a large number of different areas with a zeal that was often in inverse proportion to the logic of the reforms. Indeed in a number of cases the planned changes came to naught, either through general bafflement as to their usefulness, their sheer unworkability, or determined opposition from the people they would most affect (e.g. Cahuc and Zylberberg 2009).

But in a number of other areas there have been significant reforms, including major changes to the constitution, taxation, conditions of work and pay, retirement age, public sector pensions, trade union representation, policing, universities, the health service and the judiciary. On the whole, the reforms were characteristic of a right-wing government of the late twentieth or early twenty-first century. They tended to favour business and the wealthy at the expense of ordinary working people; to cut public expenditure and reduce the number of workers in the public sector; to restrict immigration and to reinforce state powers as far as law and order was concerned. This was certainly the main direction of the path taken by Sarkozy and his government, although the economic crisis derailed a number of measures and obliged government to introduce others. But there were, even in the early days, reforms which were less easy to place on the left-right spectrum and some that were more associated with a left-leaning agenda, including far-reaching reforms relating to the environment and climate change, or abolishing advertising on state-owned television channels, and the so-called HADOPI law which introduced new regulations regarding the internet and intellectual property. A maverick approach was also reflected in the nomination of certain ministers who were more associated with the left than the right, including former *Parti socialiste* (PS) members Bernard Kouchner as Foreign Minister and former PS national secretary Eric Besson as Minister for Immigration, Integration, National Identity and Development Solidarity. Martin Hirsch, former president of Emmaüs France, a charity working to combat poverty and homelessness, was appointed High Commissioner for Poverty Eradication, and Fadela Amara, former head of the well-known feminist organisation *Ni putes, ni soumises* ('Neither whores nor submissives', hereafter NPNS) as Junior Minister for Urban

Regeneration. This much-trumpeted approach to government was known as *ouverture*, or 'opening' to non-strictly right-wing politicians.

In a clear break with tradition among French politicians, Sarkozy's tumultuous private life not only became public knowledge but was analysed in detail by the national and (even more) by the international media, and this media attention was certainly at times used by the Sarkozy camp as a way of attempting to improve the president's political fortunes. It often had the contrary effect, however. Cécilia Sarkozy, his wife at the time of his election as president, had been the subject of much discussion because she had already had an affair with a man in New York before returning to her husband in Paris. Soon after their move to the Elysée Palace Cécilia and Sarkozy separated and he began an intense and again very public liaison with the former model and successful singer Carla Bruni, and they married in February 2008. For many, this lively personal life confirmed the lack of substance which seemed increasingly to characterise the new French presidency, and older voters in particular (many of whom had voted for Sarkozy in spring 2007) became disillusioned. Such attention to Sarkozy's private life certainly highlighted something new about his presidency beyond its undoubted trivialisation in some respects. Never before had a French politician relied so heavily on the media, with which Sarkozy had important business and personal ties, but partly because of intense media coverage of his every move, he quickly became unpopular. As early as February 2008 the new president was as unpopular as Chirac had been in February 1996 after the widespread strikes against labour reform in December 1995, with only 36 per cent of the French satisfied with Sarkozy as president (*Le Monde* 26.02.10). This was to prove to be a longer-term trend and by July 2010 he had the support of only 26 per cent of the population.

The personal problems which were aired so copiously in the media might have passed very fast if it had not been for other major obstacles of substance in the way of Sarkozy's forward march. First, those directly affected by Sarkozy's reforms often put up substantial resistance to the proposals, including transport workers, employees in the energy sector, the judiciary, teachers, students and university lecturers. Millions went on strike and millions more took to the streets in frequent days of action against new legislation and to protest against the effects of the economic crisis and the government's handling of it. But Sarkozy and his supporters had anticipated these protests and had taken pre-emptive action in the form of deluging the country with so many different reforms and of so many different types in such a short space of time that opposing them often became difficult. Important elements of the core programme were thus implemented.

Second, the economic crisis began to affect France badly during the first twelve months of Sarkozy's presidency and seriously hampered many of his initial plans. Sarkozy came to power determined to re-structure the French economy along the lines of those of the United States and Britain, including measures to deregulate the business and consumer environment, cut taxes for the rich, reduce the power of trade unions, shrink the size of the public sector and reform the labour market. By late 2007 it was of course widely recognised that (quite apart from the dire social consequences of such measures) precisely such characteristics had had a catastrophic effect on banks and other financial organisations as they had enabled and encouraged reckless and ruthless behaviour on the part of business people worldwide, but in particular in countries where the neo-liberal model prevailed. This had at least triggered the international economic crisis, even if its ultimate causes were more deep-rooted. Sarkozy and his colleagues were obliged, therefore, to perform a U-turn regarding their approach towards economic policy and Sarkozy became in his rhetoric — and to an extent in his practice — a stronger supporter of the more state-oriented capitalism for which France was known. Thus the global economic crisis has presented an additional layer of complexity in this already complex situation, particularly as many of Sarkozy's reforms were designed to deregulate aspects of the economy and stimulate free enterprise, an approach which now seems far less appropriate even to former champions of neo-liberalism. Moreover, Sarkozy had preached in favour of an 'economic and fiscal shock' which would promote growth, and he had promised to be the 'president of higher living standards'. Neither increased economic growth nor higher living standards – at least for the vast majority of the population – came about.

How, then, do we make sense of the Sarkozy phenomenon, which is apparently so fraught with ambiguity, contradiction and changes of direction? In this book I argue that the current political era is reminiscent of and usefully comparable with other episodes in French history where forceful yet maverick leaders have come to power at times of volatility and crisis and have ruled in an authoritarian fashion for a limited period. More specifically, I argue that Sarkozy's rule is best understood with principal reference to the notion of Bonapartism, which has a long history in French politics, and his approach to governing is reminiscent in particular of both de Gaulle's and that of Napoleon III. In a nutshell, Bonapartism is an exceptional form of political rule which results from an unstable situation and where an authoritarian leader steps in and appeals to the electorate in a populist fashion with promises of modernisation and progress. The notion refers to a set of underlying characteristics of rule which are common to different regimes in different eras in different circumstances, and do not by any means repeat each other exactly. The most obvious characteristics include: a highly personalised and autocratic approach to government of the country; a mix of ideological references whilst all the time speaking in terms of national salvation; a populist approach to ordinary people, attempting to appeal to them directly; intense use of the media to achieve the leader's aims; and talk of a clean break with what went before. These characteristics reflect recourse on the part of the ruling class to particular approaches to government because it sees no other possible way to achieve changes which it believes are necessary.

Certainly, there are other factors at work which help explain the nature of Sarkozy's regime. First, with his preoccupation with immigration and law and order, Sarkozy has managed to appeal to voters who have for a number of years voted for the extreme right *Front national* (FN). So there is some truth in those analysts' views who argue that he has managed to unite the right around a set of values which range from centre-right to extreme right (e.g. Dupin). Second, as I will argue in the chapters which follow, Sarkozy very much defends mainstream, conservative business interests and is intimately connected with them. Third, it should be pointed out that there is a trend in various liberal democracies for the emergence of Bonapartist—what Domenico Losurdo (2007) has described as 'soft Bonapartist'—regimes where the personality and individual characteristics of the leader are particularly pronounced and where the interest in politics on the part of the ordinary people is diminishing. Sarkozy is not altogether out of step, then, with trends in other industrialised countries, but expresses a particularly developed form of this type of rule.

I argue in this book that in order to understand Sarkozy's rule we need to analyse the nature of French politics and society more generally, with references to French history, but also to politics and liberal democracy in other countries, and indeed the nature of the politics and political economy associated with late capitalism more generally. I suggest that the Sarkozy phenomenon must be understood in the context of international trends in politics and political economy as well as specifically French developments.

The backdrop to the emergence of Sarkozy as a maverick president of the republic is the volatility of French politics over a number of years. In many advanced capitalist countries the success of the relatively stable governmental regimes has lain in the depoliticisation of the mass of ordinary people, that is the non-participation in politics in all but the most low-key political activities (mainly simply voting in national and local elections every few years) by most people. This is arguably the case in Britain, Germany, Sweden, Denmark, Norway, the Republic of Ireland, the USA, and in many other countries where the liberal democratic paradigm has taken hold alongside a fairly successful capitalist economy. In France there was for many years an unstable political situation where revolt was never far from the surface, until the presidency of François Mitterrand brought an apparently lasting social-democratic-style compromise, from the early 1980s to the mid-1990s. The compromise was clearly incomplete, however, for although the rapid decline of the Communist Party and industrial action appeared to herald the end of the Gallic predilection for revolt, the rise of the extreme right FN under the leadership of Jean-Marie Le Pen was a clear sign that profound social and political malaise had by no means disappeared. (For a more in-depth discussion of conflict and consensus in modern French politics, see Hewlett 1998.)

After Mitterrand's presidency there followed twelve years when the centre-right Jacques Chirac was president. During this period government in France slipped once more into what might be termed — comparing with the required depoliticisation, at least — low-key crisis. First, the extreme right continued to receive between 15 and 20 per cent of the national vote, won a number of seats in the European Parliament and in local elections won control of Orange, Toulon, Marignane and Vitrolles. Second, the social democratic left in the form of the PS was in disarray, unable to unite properly around either a leader or a programme. These two factors put together meant that Le Pen was able to go through to the second round of the presidential elections in 2002 and the consequence was a run-off between the widely hated FN leader and the discredited Jacques Chirac. The period 2002–07 was, then, characterised by a certain formal political stasis, led by a president of the republic widely suspected of corruption. Moreover, the very real discontent in society at large was expressed, for example, in the large and widely supported protests against labour market, tax and social security reforms, in particular in 1995 and 2006. There was also widespread unrest in the suburbs of large towns and cities, where the descendants of immigrant families (as well as more recent immigrants) lived in often very difficult circumstances, including very high unemployment, poor housing, widespread racism and police harassment.

Sarkozy did not come to power preaching peace, reconciliation and long-deferred social harmony, however. Quite the contrary. He came to power promising to change French political customs root and branch and insisting that his rule would be that of an authority figure which France so needed in order to overcome the damaging concessions made to street protests and political correctness, concessions which had, he argued, characterised the previous few decades of weak rule. Under his rule the sloppy politics of the past would be thrown out, France would once again become properly prosperous, and order would be restored to a society which had slipped gradually back into disorder.

There is, then, a conjunction of various different phenomena which need to be explored in order to understand the emergence and partial success of Sarkozy, which I will examine in the chapters that follow. First, largely as a result of the revolutionary and republican tradition, there is a repeated pattern in France for the emergence of what can now be described as Bonapartist figures, to whom the ruling class has recourse at moments of volatility when otherwise there might either be revolt from below or severely curtailed modernisation. Second, the Sarkozy version of this recurring phenomenon clearly brings with it a neo-liberal approach to economic policy, which is of course an international trend, albeit less so since the onset of the economic crisis. Third, there is increasing prevalence internationally of mediatised, celerbrity-like, strong leaders, including Thatcher, Blair, Berlusconi, Putin and Obama, as the phenomenon of politics as spectacle accompanies depoliticisation. Fourth (and related to some of these previous points), the main opposition party, the PS, has been incapable of providing a coherent alternative to the mainstream right for almost a decade. The immediate fortunes of Sarkozy and his *Union pour un mouvement populaire* (UMP) party will depend on whether the PS is able to change this situation.

Below I provide a summary of the remaining chapters in this book.

In Chapter Two I begin with a discussion regarding cycles of authoritarian rule followed by more liberal democratic regimes in modern French history. I then examine the theory of Bonapartism, with particular reference to Marx's *The Eighteenth Brumaire of Louis Bonaparte*, first published in 1852, but also to René Rémond's analysis of the Bonapartist tradition in *Les Droites en France* (*The Right Wing in France*, 1969). I examine the reasons for the emergence of and the nature of two previous autocratic and populist regimes in modern French history, namely those of Napoleon III and Charles de Gaulle. On both occasions, these leaders emerged as a result of national crisis, including crisis of political representation: Napoleon III came to power in the wake of the revolution of 1848 and de Gaulle became head of state in the midst of political and military crisis over Algeria in 1958. In each case, there were promises that the exceptional leader would bring France out of the state of decline into which the nation had sunk, and that his authoritarian rule would be of great benefit to ordinary people.

In Chapter Three I concentrate on the period leading up to the election of Sarkozy as President of the Republic and begin to examine in more detail his style, political programme and strategy. I argue that he attempted to portray France as a nation in decline that needed an exceptional leader like himself to solve the country's economic, social and (in his parlance) 'moral' problems, a country that had lost its way as far as religion, delinquency and sexual 'deviance' is concerned, as well as in the domains which are the more conventional preoccupation of politicians. In order to understand both Sarkozy's approach and the reasons it struck a certain chord in various quarters I suggest we need to look briefly at the Chirac presidency (1995–2002) and the political and industrial relations problems the president and government encountered during that period. Next, I point to the way in which Sarkozy is in some respects a conventional conservative politician who has both carefully used the party political machine in order to further his ambitions and nurtured very close ties with business, including friendships with some of the richest and most successful business people in France and elsewhere. I then look at the state of the major party-political opposition to Sarkozy, for without a certain disarray in the opposition parties — and in particular the PS — his rise to the position of president as authoritarian autocrat would have been far more difficult and probably impossible. Next I interpret the election results of spring 2007 and look closely at the fortunes of the FN, many of whose former supporters changed their allegiance to Sarkozy and were a crucial ingredient in his success. Finally, I discuss Sarkozy's approach to the legacy of the student and worker uprising of May 1968, which is highly revealing as to the more general nature of his beliefs and his strategy.

In Chapter Four I explore the period during which Sarkozy has been president. I begin by examining the tactics used by the Sarkozy regime which were largely a reaction against the perceived problems of the Chirac era and include both deluging France with planned changes in the first eighteen months (which were presented as urgent) but at the same time negotiating with interested parties and compromising on some important points. I then divide my examination of new legislation into two main areas, which I describe in the first part as the pursuit of the free economy. This included a drive to erode state protection of the labour market, undermine the 35-hour week, and introduce new fiscal benefits for the wealthy, as well as more populist measures such as abolishing taxation on mortgage interest payments and exempting students from paying tax on income. An important consideration in the realm of economic and labour reform is of course the economic crisis, which descended on France in mid- to late 2008 and hampered Sarkozy and his government's ability to continue with the mainly — although not entirely — neo-liberal agenda they were pursuing. The second area of my examination of the details of changes under Sarkozy combines a look at the reinforcing of the president as autocrat on the on hand and the construction of a stronger state on the other.

Pronounced autocratic tendencies have included not only the manic and controlling activity for which he is so well-known, and careful influence over the media in various ways, but also changes to the constitution of the Fifth Republic which were presented as enhancing the role of parliament and reducing the power of the president but which have in fact done the opposite. The state has become more repressive in various ways, such as forcibly repatriating greater numbers of illegal immigrants (*sans papiers*), breaking up traveller communities' encampments and punishing a greater number of disruptive or truant school students with the full force of the law. Finally, I look at popular opinion regarding Sarkozy and the Sarkozy regime, in particular as far as European and local elections are concerned in 2008, 2009 and 2010.

In the concluding Chapter Five I return to the question of whether the best way of explaining the Sarkozy phenomenon is by reference to the notion of Bonapartism, pointing out that Bonapartism is about both underlying conditions and governmental tactics, rather than reproducing an exact blueprint from an original model. I also raise the question of whether we should argue that Bonapartism (at least in its milder forms) should be viewed as being more prevalent than is generally thought. Such an approach does, I argue, allow us convincingly to go beyond the idea that a leader such as Sarkozy is somehow entirely at odds with the 'normal' politics of other liberal democracies (or with what preceded it in France, for that matter) and therefore a complete aberration. Instead, he and his way of governing should be seen as being on the same continuum — although at the extreme end — as trends in the nature of political leadership more generally. I also look at other interpretations of the nature of Sarkozy's rule, including that of Alain Badiou, who argues that it is a form of Pétainism, after Philippe Pétain, the leader of the Vichy regime from 1940 to 1944 and who collaborated with the Nazis. Others (especially Musso 2008) argue that Sarkozy's approach is akin to that of Berlusconi's in Italy and that there is a new phenomenon that we can call 'Sarkoberlusconism'.

Having reviewed other interpretations, however, I conclude that the most helpful way of understanding the Sarkozy's rise to power and the nature of his regime is to view this as a modern form of Bonapartism which is supported in order to achieve what otherwise seemed impossible.

Chapter Two

The Nature of Bonapartism

> [T]he class struggle in France created circumstances and relations that made it possible for a grotesque mediocrity to play a hero's part.
>
> Karl Marx on Napoleon III (Marx 1968 [1852]: 57)

In order to assess the extent to which the notion of Bonapartism enables an understanding of the rise to power and presidency of Nicolas Sarkozy, in this chapter I examine the theory and history of Bonapartism. Modern France has famously had a particularly revolutionary and turbulent history and has arguably failed to achieve lasting compromise politics. Politics has often been played out in the form of overt conflict, where popular uprisings, *coups d'état* and invasions determine the nature of national government. Many ordinary people, as well as political leaders, remained convinced that dramatic change bringing emancipation or salvation was urgently needed and periods of stability were thus relatively brief. The periods of highly authoritarian rule where a great deal of power is concentrated in the hands of one individual, then, may be seen as the main counterpart to France's history of revolution and popular revolt. On a number of occasions in the modern history of France, authoritarian and autocratic leaders have stepped in during periods of particular instability, and have won widespread support for a limited time. Napoleon I, Napoleon III, Philippe Pétain and Charles de Gaulle are among the most significant leaders of this type. At the most general level, there is room for the emergence of a leader preaching salvation through investment in their own dominance when there is a crisis of authority and an inability on the part of the existing regime to achieve stability, often involving fear of popular uprising.

Certainly, each of the leaders mentioned above emerged as a result of national emergency, including crisis of political representation: Napoleon I came to power in the Eighteenth Brumaire *coup d'état* of 1799 in the midst of military, financial and political turmoil; Napoleon III came to power in the wake of the revolution of 1848; Pétain came with the German invasion in summer 1940; and de Gaulle returned to power in the midst of the political and military impasse over Algeria in spring 1958. In each case, there were promises that the exceptional leader would save France from the crisis which it was experiencing, and that in addition to his authoritarian rule benefiting France's formal political institutions, its role on the international stage and economic wellbeing, his strong leadership and exceptional vision would be of great benefit to ordinary people, both materially and morally. Apart from the rule of Napoleon I, however, these episodes ended in each case with ordinary people rising up in one form or another.

This is not the place for a longer discussion of the general characteristics of France's conflictual and insurrection -prone history and of the explanations for these characteristics (see Hewlett 1998: 11–56), but I wish to dwell a little longer on the fact that France's history of instability and revolt is characterised by cycles consisting of (though not necessarily in this order): popular revolt; constitutionally-oriented government which attempts a greater degree of representation of ordinary voters; and rule by powerful autocrats. Thus, periods of autocratic rule have often been followed immediately by episodes where there was experimentation with direct democracy and an assertion of popular power, before partial constitutional absorption of more democratic impulses. After Napoleon III came the Paris Commune of 1871, and then the Third Republic; after Pétain came the uprisings of the years 1944–7, and then the estab-

lishment of the Fourth Republic; and towards the end of de
Gaulle's presidency came the events of May 1968. In the
aftermath of May 1968 there was a politically radical period
in the early 1970s, and then the less conflictual late 1970s
and beyond, under Presidents Valéry Giscard d'Estaing
then François Mitterrand. Anticipating the discussion
below, we might say in Gramscian terms that for many
years in modern French history there was no political
grouping that could consistently attract the level of consent
needed for a particular class to govern without fear of ongoing and substantial challenges to its political and moral
authority.

In terms of types of formal government, French political
history since the Revolution of 1789 can thus be seen as
evolving in terms of quasi-alternation between regimes
where the ordinary voter is afforded greater sway (the most
notable and durable examples of this are the Third and
Fourth Republics) and regimes which are organised around
an authoritarian, autocratic head of state (in particular
Napoleon I, Napoleon III and Pétain, as mentioned above).
The Fifth Republic under de Gaulle was a hybrid between the
two types of regime, with many characteristics of a modern
liberal democracy which were, however, combined with
both constitutionally-determined strong presidentialism
and a highly autocratically-inclined head of state. As
mentioned above, both types of regime — authoritarian-
autocratic and more liberal democratic — have tended to end
in crisis, as did de Gaulle's hybrid.

In one of the clearest general analyses of the process of
alternation between one type of regime and the other, Stanley Hoffmann discusses what he calls 'heroic leadership', or
'crisis authority', which he suggests is 'a sudden reassertion
of personal authority compared with the impersonal authority of routine periods' (Hoffmann 1967: 115–16). Writing in
particular with Pétain, Mendès-France (who was briefly
prime minister in 1954–5) and de Gaulle in mind, Hoffmann
points out, for example, that Pétain's wartime regime was
followed by the Fourth Republic, which allowed relatively
substantial influence for ordinary people via directly-elected

members of parliament and was in fact a reaction not only against Pétain but against de Gaulle as well, after de Gaulle's period as head of the provisional government between September 1944 and January 1946. Hoffmann contends that during periods of autocratic rule, by contrast with the pattern in the USA or Britain, 'normal procedures of authority ... are suspended, and crisis leadership takes on the aspects not only of a response to the challenge but a revenge against the normal procedures' (*Ibid.*: 116).

Although there is a strong sense of national emergency and a widespread view that there is no alternative, there is nevertheless, he argues, more continuity than in totalitarian states. Indeed, according to Hoffmann, one of the historical functions of the periodic emergence of the heroic leader is the avoidance of totalitarianism.

These breakdowns in already fragile routine authority allow the heroic leader, who is often an outsider, to break in and assert their fitness to govern based on heroic and patriotic deeds carried out in the past which contrast sharply with the 'impersonal, anonymous greyness of routine authority' (Hoffmann: 123). Once in power, however, such a leader has difficulty in ruling, in part because the heroic style of leadership cannot be institutionalised and the regime is therefore inherently unstable. This type of leader, then, presents himself (never yet herself) as a saviour of the nation and seeks to differentiate himself sharply from more run-of-the-mill politicians (*Ibid.:* 133) and is often impatient with more normal rules and practices; he is rebellious, defiant and non-conformist (*Ibid.:* 127). As heroic leadership is importantly a spectacle and has strong monarchic tendencies, both the world stage and the media are important elements in creating the desired image.

In explaining this oscillation between heroic leadership and 'routine' government, Hoffmann follows the sociologist Michel Crozier, who pioneered the theory of the *société bloquée*, or stalemate society, where France is portrayed as over-bureaucratised and ossified (Crozier 1970). For Hoffmann, the French style of authority, characterised by indirect methods of communication and impersonal relations between social strata, leads to this flipping between what he describes as routine government and crisis government because subordinates' resistance to their superiors and the resulting absence of innovation leads to crises when changes are driven through from above, without consent from below (Hoffmann: 116). My own analysis of this pattern will become clearer as the book progresses, but suffice it to say at this point that while there is much that is useful in Crozier's — and indeed Hoffmann's — analysis, their approach does not get to the heart of the problem. For example, Hoffmann refers to stalemate society and ineffective methods of communication as being among the root causes of the tendency for France to flip between autocratic political leadership and less leader-dominated government. But I would interpret these characteristics ('stalemate society' and so on) as being part of the results of more deep-rooted causes. In a nutshell, I prefer to talk about failure to depoliticise, as indeed does Hoffmann to an extent, commenting that de Gaulle, Mendès-France and Pétain all pursue versions of depoliticisation (*Ibid.*: 131), a notion to which we will return.

Before moving on, it is perhaps worth pointing out that many of the characteristics of heroic leadership mentioned by Hoffmann apply (at least in a superficial, weakened form, and/or as aspirations on the president's part) to the Sarkozy leadership. Despite being part of the mainstream right, in his initial presidential election campaign Sarkozy was at pains to present himself as an outsider both to mainstream politics and even to some extent to France itself (with references to non-French lineage on his father's side of the family), and that his mission was to save France from the slough of immobility into which it had sunk. He wished to send the message that he was saving France from the greyness of the previous decade under the presidency of Jacques Chirac, and even under Mitterrand in his second term of office. Next, Sarkozy certainly has a degree of difficulty ruling — another characteristic of heroic leadership identified by Hoffmann — and despite strong loyalty by many of his collaborators, extra-parliamentary opposition in particular is often ferocious, especially in relation to his more maverick attempts at new legislation, and his popularity has been consistently low in the opinion polls since late 2007. Certainly, the monarchic reference is also apt, particularly in the extreme personalisation of power, including in the constitutional reform which allows the president to address both houses of parliament each year at the Palace of Versailles. Finally, both the world stage and the media are important to Sarkozy's image as a strong leader and to the way in which he conducts himself.

Below I discuss the notion of Bonapartism as expressed by Marx and Antonio Gramsci, before examining two periods of rule which are of particular relevance to that of Sarkozy, namely the autocratic and populist regimes of Napoleon III and of Charles de Gaulle, and I argue that the more general notion of Bonapartism is useful when attempting to understand their rule. During these 'extraordinary' times when much faith is placed in the figure of one particular leader, this arrangement becomes possible because certain sections of the social, political and economic elite deem it necessary to invest power in this leader in order to drive through particular changes. Moreover, the more direct, democratic influence exerted by ordinary people at other times is weakened and is replaced by a populist arrangement where there is often support for the leader's actions and even hero worship (when there seems to be no alternative and in order to overcome the period of crisis) but very much reduced influence on the actual shape of politics from ordinary people. This is partly why these periods tend to end with a resurgence of direct influence on the part of ordinary people, in the form of popular uprising.

The extent to which these sorts of arrangements apply to Sarkozy will be explored in subsequent chapters.

Bonapartism: Marx and Gramsci

Although the more general use of the term Bonapartism is often associated with analysis from the left, both Marxist and some non-Marxist analysts have suggested that there is in French politics a long history of Bonapartism, running back to Napoleon I, but perhaps more particularly to Napoleon III, and including the rule of Charles de Gaulle. In *The Eighteenth Brumaire of Louis Bonaparte*, first published in 1852, Marx explores how Napoleon III ruled by concentrating power in the executive wing of the state, which he controlled, and weakening the legislative wing, particularly after the *coup d'état* of 2 December 1851 (Marx 1968 [1852]). For both Marx and Engels (who also found Bonapartist elements in Bismarck's rule in Germany), Bonapartism is an exceptional form of political rule which results from an unstable situation where neither the ruling class nor the working class is able to assert sufficient authority, and where an authoritarian leader steps in and claims to speak for all classes. From a non-Marxist perspective, René Rémond suggests in his classic *Les Droites en France* (*The Right Wing in France*) that there are three main currents on the right in France, namely the liberal-conservative Orleanist, the extreme-right counter-revolutionary, and the Bonapartist current. He argues that Gaullism is — or at least was under de Gaulle — strongly imbued with elements of Bonapartism, which were, notably: a personalised cult of authority; a strong state; a claim to rally the French people as a whole, from whom its authority is derived via universal suffrage; a strong modernising impulse; national independence and grandeur, especially with regard to foreign policy; and an association of capital and labour (Rémond 1982: 322–33).

One of the essential messages of Marx's *Eighteenth Brumaire* is that Bonapartism is a phenomenon which reflects a moment in mid-nineteenth-century France when many ordinary people had entered the political arena but where any real class compromise had not been achieved. Marx analyses the many paradoxes and contradictions of the first few years of Napoleon III's rule, examining the interaction between the political and the socio-economic in a way that takes on board the importance of the individual leader. On the one hand, the interests of the bourgeoisie are clear. Bonaparte's method of ruling can only be understood in light of the 1848 revolution, which terrified the bourgeoisie, a class which 'had a true insight into the fact that all the weapons which it had forged against feudalism turned their points against itself' (Marx 1968: 131); their immediate response to 1848 was the savage repression of the June days, when several thousand insurgents were killed and many thousands more were deported. The conservative and largely monarchist Party of Order, which dominated parliament, paved the way for the *coup*, in part by introducing a law which abolished universal male suffrage; to be eligible to vote it was now necessary to have lived for three years in the same commune, which meant that itinerant or semi-itinerant workers in the building industry and those involved in the construction of the rapidly-expanding railway network were particularly affected. Almost three million voters out of a total nine million were disenfranchised in this way (Lentz 1995: 45). Also, a draconian new press law suppressed revolutionary newspapers and declared that no newspaper which dealt with political or economic issues could be set up without permission from the government. Thus according to Marx the law of 31 May 1850 was the bourgeoisie's own *coup d'état* (Marx 1968: 134) and this class certainly looked to Bonaparte to defend its interests and approved of the actual *coup d'état* of 2 December 1851 and the abolition of parliament. The international bourgeoisie supported Louis-Napoleon as well, and Marx quotes *The Economist*, which sums up the situation on the eve of the *coup* by saying: 'The President is the guardian of order, and is now recognised as such on every Stock Exchange of Europe' (*Ibid.*: 156).

However, according to Marx, Bonaparte's *coup* is no simple victory for the bourgeoisie and indeed he suggests that his method of government was the only possible one given the profound political crisis into which France had sunk, where 'the bourgeoisie had already lost — and the working class had not yet acquired — the capacity to govern the nation' (*Ibid.*: 162). Thus Bonapartism reflects a situation of quasi-equilibrium between principal antagonistic classes and although ultimately it serves the interests of the dominant classes it does not seem to spring from them and indeed draws its support from a part of the dominated classes. So just before the *coup* Napoleon promised he would bring a calmer future, but for the bourgeoisie Bonaparte's dictatorship was also the end of its own rule (*Ibid.*: 164–5), and although the bourgeoisie believed only Bonaparte could save bourgeois society, '[t]he struggle seems to be settled in such a way that all classes, equally impotent and equally mute, fall on their knees before the rifle butt' (*Ibid.*: 168). Marx goes on to describe Napoleon's 'confused groping, which seeks now to win, now to humiliate first one class and then another' and suggests that he wants to appear as the 'patriarchal benefactor of all classes' (*Ibid.*: 176–7). Thus Marx argues that although ultimately Napoleon III was acting in the interests of the bourgeoisie, not least by keeping the revolution at bay, the crisis meant that the bourgeoisie had to put its direct political interests to one side in order to reduce the risk of revolution. This was so much the case that during the first period after the *coup* of 2 December 1851 the state 'seem[ed] to have made itself completely independent' (*Ibid.*: 170), a view that has generated much debate among students of Marx. Certainly, the *Eighteenth Brumaire* seems to suggest that the class struggle had become so intense that it had to be partially suspended by the bourgeoisie in order to save bourgeois dominance and pre-empt revolution.

In terms of formal support via suffrage, Marx argues that Napoleon III depended on a large number of conservative peasant farmers, isolated from one another by their mode of production, incapable of forming a coherent, conscious class able to defend its interests, and which needed to be represented by and recognise themselves in him because of the clarity and evocative nature of Napoleonic memories in the countryside (*Ibid.*: 113). In fact, although many votes for Napoleon came from rural areas, support was more cross-class than Marx suggests and many people living in towns and cities also supported him (e.g. Watkins 2002: 164), which if anything further underlines the extraordinary nature of Bonapartism and the fact that it arises at moments of socio-political impasse. However, Marx's essay also foreshadows liberal-democratic politics where universal suffrage is firmly established and where politicisation is greatly reduced, and where government can often appear far less partial. Bonapartism thus embodies a tension between politicisation and de-politicisation, an idea to which I will return when discussing Sarkozy.

The notion of Bonapartism as defined by Marx has been used and adapted by several notable Marxist leaders and intellectuals in more recent times. Lenin, for example, described Kerensky, the Russian prime minister in the provisional government, as Bonapartist shortly before the October revolution in 1917 (Lenin 1977). Trotsky used the notion in the early 1930s in order to analyse the rise of fascism in Europe (notably Mussolini and Hitler), which he described as 'Bonapartism of fascist origin' and wrote of the 'senile Bonapartism' of Marshal Pétain (Trotsky 1940). (For an overview see Baehr and Richter 2004: 16–22.) But perhaps the most useful treatment of Bonapartism by Marxists in the twentieth century is by Gramsci, who often uses the term 'Caesarism' instead of 'Bonapartism' and who adapts it and explains it in such a way that the term becomes, if anything, even more powerful in his hands. One of the most important concepts in Gramsci's writings is that of hegemony, where, put simply, the ruling class is able to rule via consent of the mass of people as well as via coercion, which the more classically Marxist (and Marxist-Leninist) approach tends to emphasise. This Gramscian analysis creates, among many other things, a more subtle view of the role of the modern state, including an ideological one, which has been influential for a large number of analysts in the twentieth and twenty-first centuries. Hegemony, then, is the opposite of pure political dictatorship and is an approach to ruling whereby consent is achieved by making the economic and other interests of a particular class or sub-class into more general perceived interests, so that support is generated from many different sorts of socio-economic groups. So

> hegemony presupposes that account be taken of the interests and the tendencies of the groups over which hege-

mony is to be exercised, and that a certain compromise equilibrium should be formed — in other words, that the leading group should make sacrifices of an economic-corporate kind. But there is little doubt that that such sacrifices and such a compromise cannot touch the essential ... (Gramsci 1971: 161)

When this system of rule which includes a strong element of hegemony breaks down, and the 'ruling class has lost its consensus, i.e. is no longer "leading" but only "dominant", exercising coercive force alone', the situation becomes extremely volatile and the entire balance of forces is in danger from potential widespread revolt (*Ibid.*: 275–6). In this situation, the opposing forces are also active, a situation which Gramsci describes elsewhere as 'war of manoeuvre' (as opposed to the more stable 'war of position') and these forces are equally matched. A governmental gap is created into which can step a leader who claims to embody salvation and who typically gains support of those with vested interests in the old order:

At a certain point in their historical lives, social classes become detached from their historical parties. In other words, the traditional parties in that particular organisational form, with the particular men who constitute, represent and lead them, are no longer recognised by their class (or fraction of a class) as its expression. When such crises occur, the immediate situation becomes delicate and dangerous, because the field is wide open for violent solutions, for the activities of unknown forces, represented by charismatic 'men of destiny' ... the content is the crisis of the ruling class's hegemony, which occurs either because the ruling class has failed in some major political undertaking for which it has requested, or forcibly extracted, the consent of the broad masses (war, for example), or because huge masses (especially of peasants and petit-bourgeois intellectuals) have passed suddenly from a state of political passivity to a certain activity, and put forward demands which taken together, albeit not organically formulated, add up to a revolution. A 'crisis of authority' is spoken of: this is precisely the crisis of hegemony, or general crisis of the State. (Gramsci 1971: 210)

For Gramsci, then, Caesarism is 'the fusion of an entire social class under a single leadership' (*Ibid.*: 211), where it

seems that the alternative is destruction of that class's dominance, but where the revolutionary elements are not so
strong as to be irresistible (*Ibid.*: 211). Gramsci had in mind
in particular the rise of fascism in Europe, and especially in
his native Italy, but he also took a broader historical view
and believed that Caesarism did not always have the same
political hue. There could, he argued, be both progressive
and reactionary forms of Caesarism, depending on which
direction the strong leader led their country's government:
Caesar himself and Napoleon I were examples of progressive Caesarism, whereas Napoleon III and Bismarck were
examples of reactionary Caesarism (*Ibid.*: 219). The differ-
ences between society and politics today and society and
politics in Gramsci's — still more Marx's — time are of course
immense. But I shall argue that the notion of Bonapartism is
still highly relevant, in part because it does indeed help
explain political circumstances where the existing order
does seem to be systematically contested, but where a
strong leader manages to step in and rule for a certain
period. In today's more complex socio-economic and political circumstances where, for example, the relationship
between social class and politics is often more difficult to
ascertain, the subtle analysis offered by an approach which
has reference to Bonapartism can be most useful.

Napoleon III

Certain aspects of the first few years of Louis-Napoleon's
rule go to the heart of the complexity and paradoxes of the
particular blend of authoritarian populism that are so
strongly associated with Bonapartism. In the presidential
election of 10 December 1848, his popularity was such that
5.4 million votes were cast in his favour, compared with 1.4
million for his main rival, Cavaignac, who had put down
the revolt in June in the most brutal manner. Under the
terms of the constitution Louis was to be president for four
years and during the first few years he expended a great
deal of energy establishing and consolidating a reputation
as an authoritarian and autocratic ruler, sometimes aided

by and sometimes against the will of the majority in the National Assembly, and always justified by the need to combat the ever-present threat of the 'red peril'; to replace the period of disorder with a future overseen by a regime of profound order. Many socialist leaders were forced into exile within a matter of months, army officers loyal to Bonaparte were placed in key posts and the president began plotting the detail of the *coup d'etat* which became almost inevitable. In what was a nearly bloodless *coup* on 2 December 1851, 26,000 rank-and-file republicans were arrested, as were various parliamentary leaders (including Cavaignac and Thiers) and the National Assembly was dissolved. A new constitution was put to the electorate in the plebiscite of 20 December which gave a great deal of power to the executive and was based on the constitution of Year VIII of the Revolution (that is the constitution Napoleon I introduced in 1799). It won 7.5 million votes, with under three quarters of a million voting against and Napoleon thus not only became the supreme leader of the nation but could once again claim widespread popular support. Almost exactly a year later, the empire was established and again its establishment was approved by plebiscite with an overwhelming majority. (Plessis 1985; Lentz 1995: 49)

In addition to the support offered by the French social, economic and political elite, Napoleon III's success is explained by the more popular reputation he had created around himself during exile, which may be summed up by reference to his various writings. In his *Political Reveries*, published in 1832, he writes in favour of a revolutionary political culture and the democratic ideas expressed in the constitution of 1793, insisting that 'the democratic republic will be my cult; I will be its priest' (in Milza 2006: 753). Then in his *Napoleonic Ideas* published in 1839, a year before his uncle's ashes were brought back to Paris, he again writes in favour of a radically democratic form of republicanism, with a strong plebiscitary streak. Increasingly, then, modern Bonapartism is portrayed by Louis as an ideology where the leader is the incarnation of the people, where popular participation in politics takes the form of plebiscite, and where intermediary bodies between the leader and the led are rejected.

In his widely-read pamphlet entitled *The Extinction of Pauperism*, first published in 1844, Louis-Napoleon draws on the ideas of utopian socialists Louis Blanc and Saint-Simon and goes to some lengths to express his commitment to improving the lot of ordinary people, without however questioning the legitimacy of capitalism. In a deliberate attempt to win over workers and peasants, he argues that '[i]ndustry devours its children and lives only through their death' and '[t]he working class owns nothing; it must be made property-owning' (in Lentz 1995: 39). This pamphlet was certainly not advocating a socialist future; defence of private property, the need for order and the importance of the authoritarian leader were sentiments which were very much still there. But its socially-oriented content, strong defence of universal male suffrage and of course its campaigning title helped create a landslide victory for its author in the election in December 1848. Louis was far more confident that the elite would support him, and *The Extinction of Pauperism* was part of the campaign to gain more widespread support. To this end, it went through six editions in the years 1844–8 and extracts were distributed free of charge by Louis' supporters.

Historians of the Second Empire usually divide Napoleon III's rule into two main periods: the authoritarian period up to the beginning of the 1860s and the more liberal period during the 1860s. In the earlier period in particular, newspapers were often censored or banned, police were omnipresent and public gatherings were prohibited. In the 1860s Louis liberalised press laws, relaxed legislation regarding public gatherings and even granted the right to strike. (Lentz 1995: 74; Milza 2006: 494)

In some respects, then, Napoleon III was a defender of social liberalism and aspects of what we might now describe as liberal democracy. He was, for example, the first president to be elected by universal male suffrage. Certainly, his close Saint-Simonian advisors encouraged a certain distribution of the fruits of economic growth and the need to improve the lot of the working classes and there were some social measures, or at least state paternalism, such as worker housing and soup kitchens. There was also the idea that popular consent was necessary in order to achieve political stability. He even claimed at one point to be socialist and indeed Proudhon once suggested that the first few years of his rule were socialist (Milza 2006: 489).

However, the repression exercised by the regime in its quest for order and the guarantee of certain conditions of life and business for the ruling and business elite was also often considerable. The 1851 *coup d'état* was the outstanding example of this approach and, although the *coup* was carried out without widespread loss of life, it was nonetheless a classic repressive and authoritarian politico-military manoeuvre and many opponents were imprisoned or deported in its wake. Moreover, the regime was characterised by intense police activity and especially widespread interventions by a highly developed and active secret police, not to mention close control of the media, for example.

In the realm of economics and business, the Second Empire was a period of enormous change, led by a strong state but where the market economy was vital. Cheap credit became one of the engines of growth and transformation, and the modern banking system was established with the birth of such giants as *Crédit industriel et commercial* (1859), *Crédit lyonnais* (1863) and *Société générale* (1864). The expansion of the rail network is one of the best indicators both of economic growth and modernising zeal during this period: it grew from 3,600 kilometres of track in 1850 to 23,300 kilometres in 1870 (*Ibid.*: 95). In part Saint-Simonian in inspiration, with the glorification of industry and banking at its heart, France under Napoleon III nevertheless saw little of Saint-Simon's preoccupation with progressive social change. Although the expanding urban working classes were particularly important to the economic modernisation process, neither they nor the rural poor benefitted to any real extent. Even the relatively sympathetic Pierre Milza (*Ibid.*: 488) comments that 'the effect of applying Saint-Simonian ideas to economic management was to enrich a minority of privileged people and to consolidate bourgeois dominance'. Milza (*Ibid.*: 492) goes on to argue that:

> [a]s long as Napoleon III was content with improving the living and working conditions of the working class with measures that did not threaten the economic interests of the privileged classes, the employers let him carry on. All they needed was for the regime to guarantee social peace by muzzling the most radical opponents and by exercising careful surveillance on potential trouble-makers or supposed trouble-makers.

Many large towns and cities changed greatly during the Second Empire, including Lyon, Marseille and Bordeaux, but the transformation of Paris expresses particularly clearly some of the most important aspects of the nature of the regime. When Louis Napoleon came to power in December 1848 it was in the immediate aftermath of the revolution of 1848, which in France had its epicentre in Paris and which in June had ended in a bloodbath in the capital. The transformation of Paris was one of Louis Napoleon's major priorities and, under the immediate direction of Baron Haussmann, the city underwent the most comprehensive change of its history and this constituted one of the most radical transformations of any city in the modern world. The goals of this transformation were multiple and most importantly included: facilitation of transport of labour and goods both into and out of the city, and across the city; clearing some of the central areas, including the Ile de la Cité, of poor, working class housing and generally moving the lower classes to the north east of the city; enabling the circulation of air in order to combat cholera (which had killed 20,000 Parisians in the epidemic of 1832, for example (Marchand 1993: 27)) and other diseases; creating a national and international business centre which was suitable (as regards comfortable living and and appeal to wealthy visitors) for the economic boom which France was experiencing; facilitating the movement of troops around the city in order to put down revolt; and sweeping away the winding, narrow streets which were easy to barricade and which allowed escape from advancing troops. The results of

this transformation were mixed, but overall they undoubtedly greatly favoured the wealthy at the expense of the
working class. Certainly, the newly-opened or improved
public parks were to the benefit of all, and the greatly
increased network of boulevards also provided the oppor-
tunity for leisure activities for all social classes. But one of
the main effects of the transformations was to drive home
the message that the centre of Paris was now the place of res-
idence of the better off, especially on the tree-lined boulevards with expensive apartment buildings with facades
and street furniture conceived with the greatest care, down
to the last detail. Many members of the working classes who
were displaced and moved from the centre to often appall-
ing living conditions in the suburbs of Paris, lived in make-
shift shanty towns, with highly insanitary conditions, and
this neglect which was to contribute towards creating the
'red belt', communist-supporting suburbs in the twentieth
century. Soon after Louis Napoleon's defeat and capture at
Sedan at the hands of the Prussians, the eruption of the Paris
Commune in early 1871 was in part a reaction of the Parisian working class to the previous two decades of socially
prejudiced upheaval in the capital.

To conclude and sum up this brief examination of relevant aspects of the rule of Napoleon III, I will again quote
the emperor himself. Louis edited a *History of Julius Caesar*,
the first volume of which appeared in 1865, and in whose
preface he alluded to the recent history of France, pointing
out that Caesar demanded strong government 'capable of
re-establishing order and social peace after more than sev-
enty years of anarchy and struggles'. Louis no doubt had his
government and in particular himself in mind, as well as
Caesar, as he wrote these words, as he did when he wrote a
little later in the same text:

> In order to establish a lasting order it was necessary to find
> a man who, rising above vulgar passions, had the essential
> qualities and the correct ideas of each of his predecessors,
> whilst avoiding both their defects and their errors. To gen-
> erosity of spirit and a love of the people it was necessary to
> add the military genius of the great generals and the dicta-

tor's profound sense of order and hierarchy. (In Milza 2006: 756)

As Milza points out, this was — apart from the mention of 'military genius', which is more appropriate in reference to his uncle — a description which Louis-Napoleon penned with himself very much in mind, as well as Julius Caesar.

De Gaulle

History never repeats itself exactly, of course, as Marx famously points out in the opening passage of *The Eighteenth Brumaire*, but General de Gaulle's presidency between 1958 and 1969 bore sufficient resemblances to the regime of Napoleon III to be described usefully as Bonapartist. Perhaps most obviously, de Gaulle ruled in highly autocratic fashion. His personalised power was made possible in part because of the circumstances under which he came to power, during military and political crisis, when in May 1958 important sections of the army were preparing a *coup d'etat* in reaction to perceived betrayal by the politicians in Paris over the crisis in colonial Algeria. For this reason, de Gaulle's army-supported accession to the position of head of state is itself sometimes described as a *coup d'etat*, although *quasi-coup d'etat* is probably a more accurate description, as de Gaulle's return to politics did not involve military manoeuvres to install him in the Elysée Palace. His return to power did, however, benefit greatly from the knowledge that he commanded the army's respect and that without this support the situation would have been even more dangerous. De Gaulle thus came to power as saviour, after a period of profound turmoil and he ruled as if he alone could enable France to survive intact. A new political constitution was introduced in order to enable formal legislative support for the president's own style of government, which I discuss below.

In terms of popularity and populism de Gaulle's rule was also reminiscent of Louis Napoleon's, in that his support base in the population at large was fairly broad-based and cross-class, particularly in the early years of his rule. In addition to regular elections (including, in 1965, the first presidential election by universal suffrage since 1848) where de Gaulle and his supporters fared well, he organised a total of five referenda (four in the first five years), which were as much plebiscite-like consultations seeking approval for his autocratic rule as enquiries into the views of the French on particular issues. In each referendum, there were threats of de Gaulle's departure if the result went against his wishes, and on each occasion apart from the last (in 1969) he won a clear majority. In April 1969, less than a year after the May 1968 uprising which he appeared to have so badly misunderstood, he submitted some fairly minor elements of constitutional reform to the voters via referendum. He warned of mayhem in the event of a No vote, which would trigger his immediate departure from office:

> How, then, will the situation be brought under control – a state of affairs resulting from the negative victory of all those diverse, disparate, discordant and opposing forces, with the inevitable return to the rule of ambitions, illusions, alliances and betrayals – in the national disorder that such a breakdown will provoke? (De Gaulle 1970: 406)

The majority of voters did on that occasion have the courage to vote against de Gaulle and he resigned as soon as the result was declared.

Such Bonapartist *coups de théâtre* were entirely characteristic of de Gaulle's rule, but so were other, less dramatic tendencies which were just as Bonapartist. A brief look at the constitution of the Fifth Republic will remind us that the formal context within which parliamentary and presidential politics have been operating since 1958 is one which has a strong Bonapartist orientation and that the constitution provides a suitable framework for the construction and consolidation of personalized power. (For longer treatments see, for example, Berstein and Rudelle 1992; Volpi 1979.) Olivier Duhamel (1993: 181) comments that de Gaulle's most important idea about the constitution was that 'it goes without saying that government should not stem from Parliament'. According to de Gaulle, the supposed excessive power of the lower house over the composition and programme of government under the Fourth Republic that was the main cause of instability; more effective government, on the other hand, would rely on a constitution which gave government and the president far more autonomy from and power over the legislature. The Fifth Republic does indeed allow for a great deal of executive (presidential and governmental) power and relatively little parliamentary power. The president is elected by universal suffrage (this was an amendment to the constitution introduced – by referendum – in 1962) and is responsible for the choice of prime minister and his or her dismissal, and he (never yet she) nominates the rest of the cabinet in consultation with the prime minister. The president may submit proposed changes in legislation to the French people in the form of a referendum and may dissolve the *Assemblée nationale*, thus provoking an election.

The most controversial presidential power of all is described in Article 16, which allows the head of state 'exceptional powers' (defined very generally as being those 'required by the circumstances') for a certain period during a time of crisis. This provision has been used only once since 1958, by de Gaulle, between 23 April and 30 September 1961 after a *putsch* by four generals in Algeria, during which period de Gaulle ruled by decree. But it is a highly significant provision in that it is a symbol of the power of the president and is always there, to be used if necessary. Although the constitution gives substantial powers to the president there is nevertheless a degree of ambiguity which allows room for interpretation. Although the president chairs cabinet meetings, the government 'determines and conducts the policy of the nation' (Article 20) and 'directs the action of government' (Article 21), and although the president is military leader (Article 15), the government 'is in charge of the administration of the armed forces' (Article 20) and the prime minister is 'responsible for the defense of the nation' (Article 21). In the text, then, it is nowhere clearly laid out who actually governs, but in practice it has been the presidents of the republic who have dominated the legislature, the government, the civil service, the judiciary, the army, foreign policy and defence. This dominance prompted Maurice Duverger (1974) to call the Fifth Republic a 'republican monarchy'.

The constitution itself, then, has strong Bonapartist leanings, which Mitterrand described in his book published in 1962, entitled *Le coup d'état permanent*, although when Mitterrand became president of the republic in 1981 he made no attempt at radical reform of the constitution. But the constitution also contains more liberal democratic elements, in a blend which closely reflects de Gaulle's own politics.

Just as importantly, de Gaulle's regime put state-led economic modernisation at the top of its agenda. Reminiscent of the situation in the Second Empire where Napoleon III's rule must be explained by reference to the 1848 revolution and the continued threat of revolution, the powerful Communist Party (which still typically attracted one in five voters) and the dominant *Confédération générale du travail* (CGT), communist-oriented trade union confederation, reflected the enduring radicalism of the organised working class, balanced by the equally intransigent *patronat*. The threat of popular armed insurrection was no longer present in the 1960s, but class conflict was still an obstacle to capitalist modernisation, and de Gaulle's *dirigiste* approach to economic modernisation and highly personalised and top-down approach to government was intended to help overcome the immense obstacles presented by this intense class conflict.

Political stability under de Gaulle created the conditions for substantial economic modernisation. Certainly, under the Fourth Republic there had already been significant economic growth, increases in productivity, rural exodus and increases in the standard of living for many. But in 1958 France remained behind many of its main competitors according to the classic indicators, including investment as a proportion of GDP, size of firms, and prevalence of family- or individually-owned firms. Trade was still mainly oriented towards France's colonies or ex-colonies and exports generally were comparatively weak (e.g. Braudel and Labrousse 1982; Jeanneney 1992). De Gaulle zealously pursued state-led, top-down economic change. Economic planning on the part of the state, already important in the post-war period became in the words of de Gaulle an 'ardent necessity' (de Gaulle 1970: 171–2) and planning in the 1960s offered huge stimulus to key industrial sectors (chemicals, consumer electronics, steel, motor cars, telecommunications and so on) and mergers of smaller firms were greatly encouraged. This *dirigiste* approach to economic change depended upon a highly centralised state, which involved a reinforcing of the administrative elite, which was fed by graduates from the *grandes écoles*, particularly the *Ecole nationale d'administration* (ENA), founded in 1945 by de Gaulle's close associate Michel Debré.

Many of the key aims of de Gaulle's economic policy were indeed realised by the end of the 1960s, including growth of GDP, a higher rate of investment, greatly increased exports, with far more trade than previously with other industrialised countries, and a concentration on other EU member states. In a favourable international economic climate, France managed to outstrip almost all competitors as far as conventional indicators are concerned. However, this top-down approach to economic modernisation meant the fruits of greater prosperity were very unevenly distributed and certain sectors of the population remained greatly disadvantaged during these years. For example, the minimum wage, *Salaire minimum interprofessionnel de croissance* (SMIC) rose only 71 per cent between 1955 and 1967, compared with 156 per cent for blue-collar wages as a whole (Berstein 1989: 121). Moreover, industrial relations often remained archaic at the end of the 1960s, with no or virtually no collective bargaining in many small and medium-sized firms. The highly uneven Gaullist economic modernisation programme, then, reminiscent indeed of that of Louis Napoleon, helps explain the uprising and three-week general strike of May 1968.

During de Gaulle's presidency, a particularly graphic manifestation of the insecurity of the ruling class and the unevenness of political modernisation was the persistent brutality of the police. Most tragically, between a hundred and two hundred Algerians were killed by police in Paris on the night of 17–18 October 1961, after 20,000 Algerians had marched through Paris in protest against a curfew imposed on them. A few months later, on 8 February 1962, eight participants in a demonstration against the anti-Algerian independence *Organisation de l'armée secrète* were killed and over one hundred injured in charges by police at the Paris metro station Charonne. This is not to mention the police violence in May 1968, which although causing relatively few deaths, was systematic and played an important part in uniting students and workers in their revolt against aspects of Gaullism.

In the realm of foreign policy as well, there were important aspects of de Gaulle's rule that were distinctly Bonapartist. He regarded this domain as crucial to his historical mission and summed up his view of France's proper role in world affairs as one of *grandeur*. It was a domain for which de Gaulle took responsibility almost single-handedly, including the highly controversial process of granting formal independence to Algeria after many years of war against the independence movement. Both in relation to the construction of the European Union and participation in NATO de Gaulle took a wary position on behalf of France, arguing that such supranational organisations were a threat to the country's sovereignty. The development of the *Force de frappe* nuclear deterrent was designed to underline France's independence and importance on the world stage, as was a certain diplomatic distance from both the USA and the USSR. In practice – at least in its detail – foreign relations under de Gaulle perhaps involved little that was very different from the foreign relations of many other advanced capitalist countries of the time. But in terms of ideology it meant far more and arguably helped enable de Gaulle to achieve a certain temporary unity of purpose among many French people with domestic issues in mind as well as foreign relations. In other words, foreign policy helped to bind the nation together and distract attention from serious inequalities and conflicts of interest which could have – and indeed in the end did – produce grave discontent and revolt on the part of some groups in French society. All this was approached with the figure of de Gaulle in the position of supreme leader.

Conclusions

Different circumstances throw up different versions of Bonapartism and some would indeed dispute that there are enough similarities between, say, the rule of Napoleon III and that of de Gaulle to allow us to call Gaullism Bonapartist. However, I contend that there are indeed striking similarities and that we can summarise the main elements of Bonapartism in the following way. An authoritarian but charismatic leader is able to rule with an unusual degree of popularity for a relatively short period of time within the framework of a strong state and with claims to being above party politics. He or she is populist, with electoral appeal across classes, a situation made possible in part by disarray among other political forces. The discourse of Bonapartism tends to be of nationalism and national unity, of modernisation and progress while conserving all that is seen as valuable in the past, and with nods in the direction of equality. The circumstances which bring a Bonapartist leader to power and allow them to rule are exceptional, or characterised by crisis, and the threat of return to crisis or instability if the leader departs. The heroic leader himself is typically an outsider who comes in to offer salvation from otherwise certain disaster; order in the face of chaos.

Certainly, the classic cases of Bonapartism — when Napoleon I and Napoleon III were heads of state — are of course the purest forms and it is possible to argue that more modern versions lack certain important elements which were found in the original forms. But it goes without saying that no two political regimes are identical. The point is to examine different cases and to decide whether the goals and/or methods of more modern regimes are similar in important ways and whether the underlying causes are also similar. This is the spirit in which we will examine both the rise to power and also the presidential rule of Sarkozy in the next two chapters.

Chapter Three

Achieving Supremacy

… most of all I wanted to describe to you the values on which my project is founded. These are work, authority, honesty, fraternity and the greatness of France. For years now politicians have not dared speak of these values, but I want to restore them to the heart of French political life. They will serve to guide my actions for the next five years if you elect me President of the Republic.

Nicolas Sarkozy, *Mon Projet. Ensemble, tout devient possible*
(Sarkozy 2007b: 4)

In Chapter Two I explored the theory and practice of Bonapartism and looked in particular at the regimes of Napoleon III and de Gaulle. In this chapter and Chapter Four I examine the rise to high office and the presidency of Nicolas Sarkozy and argue that there are strong Bonapartist characteristics in both the style and substance of Sarkozy's rule, which include: a highly personalised and autocratic approach to government of the country; a mix of ideological references while all the time speaking in terms of national salvation; a populist approach to relations with the French people, attempting to appeal directly to ordinary people; intense use of the media to achieve his aims; and talk of a clean break with what went before. We have seen that Bonapartism is a highly complex phenomenon, which often arises when there is an impasse — or perceived impasse — on the part of the ruling elite and its allies.

In order to understand Sarkozy's electoral success we need to look both at what were seen as problems on the part of certain sections of the political and business elite, the state of the mainstream left and at the nature of Sarkozy's ideas and campaign for the presidency. After a discussion of the image which was built around the figure of Sarkozy, I examine certain crucial ways in which the Chirac presidency was seen to fail. I then look at the way in which Sarkozy described the state that France was in and the reasons why the country needed someone with his exceptional credentials who was offering salvation. Next, I examine the way in which he – in more conventional fashion – used the new party of the right (the UMP), his strong business connections and the media in order to further his ambitions. I then look at the recent history of the mainstream left, in particular the PS, in order to help understand why Sarkozy's appeal among the electorate was relatively broad. We are then in a better position to interpret the elections of 2007 which brought Sarkozy to power. I also give special attention both to Sarkozy's approach towards the FN and to his obsession with the nature and legacy of the uprising of May 1968.

An important part of my argument is that although a large section of the natural supporters of the right – and in particular the business community – favoured a thorough 'neo-liberalisation' of the French economy, it was clear that this was not going to be achieved easily and in particular not via open and frontal confrontation with those who had the most to lose from such a transformation. Rather, it would – this was at least the gamble – be achieved by investing in a maverick autocrat who was not a straight-forward and conventional man of the mainstream right, but one who appeared to have qualities which would allow modernisation using unusual methods. As we shall see in both this chapter and in the one that follows, Sarkozy came with an aspiration to effect revolution (or more accurately counter-revolution) in many domains, but in particular in those which may be broadly described as work, law and order and immigration.

An exceptional leader for a failing nation?

The carefully constructed image of Sarkozy that was presented to the French electorate was one of a man who had special insight into the problems the country suffered, combined with unique drive and inspiration with regard to how to solve them. Despite this, the image was in some respects, and quite deliberately, one of a very ordinary person. The son of an impoverished and estranged Hungarian father (albeit an aristocrat who had fallen on hard times) and a French mother, Sarkozy had been an unremarkable school and university student without outstanding academic achievements. Some of his well-aired tastes and inclinations also suggest a man of the people rather than a bourgeois who was privileged by birth and education; he likes to listen to the music of Johnny Hallyday and to watch television; he cycles and he plays football; and he makes no claim to be widely read. He rose in the world of law and business, he explains, not because of who he was and who he knew, but as a result of hard work and dedication. The same applies, or so the myth surrounding him goes, to his political career, which was also one of a self-made man. This image of a man who understands the ordinary person but who also has special leadership qualities was ever-present in the long campaign to become president and he went out of his way to portray himself as a determined, ruthlessly ambitious man of action with boundless energy. All this is expressed clearly in the opening passage of his best-selling book, *Témoignage* ('Testimony'):

> As far back as I can remember, I have always wanted to take action. I've always had a passion for transforming the mundane, making the impossible seem possible, finding room for manoeuvre. Politics was not a family tradition, quite the contrary; I had neither contacts nor money, I was not a civil servant and I had a name which, because it sounded foreign, would have persuaded many people to disappear into anonymity. But politics for me was uniquely interesting and drew me to work with other French people, not against them, and not without them. I like the idea of action with others, towards a common objective and in order to give hope to millions of people. I want to explain here that no-one should be put off if they are prepared to be daring, to strive and to be ambitious. I love to build, to act and to solve problems. I believe that one can always achieve and that in the end effort always pays

off. These are my values. That is why I am involved in politics, that is what justifies, in my view, achieving the highest
level of responsibility. (Sarkozy 2006: 1)

This is a portrait of a single-minded man who, crucially,
has got where he is through hard work. Just as importantly,
ambitious though he is, he is keen to bring others with him
and allow them a share of the benefits of the common plan,
as long as they work hard and remain loyal.

There was thus a profound personalisation of politics in
the run-up to the elections of 2007, and the image he presented was of someone who not only offered the political
solutions to France's woes but had first-hand experience of
both the nation's problems and the necessary solutions. He
himself had worked hard and was a successful business-
man and lawyer. He was also partially of immigrant origin
but — by implicit contrast with many immigrants and their
descendants — he loved France and had contempt for those
who did not, or appeared not to. During the 2007 election
campaign it became clear that Sarkozy was making the election more plebiscitary in nature than any others had been
since de Gaulle, a contest that if he won he would interpret
as a mandate to rule in highly autocratic fashion. At every
rally, in every television appearance, every interview and
press release, he built the image of himself as personal
bearer of the formula necessary to bring France out of the
moral decline, political lethargy and economic crisis into
which he said it had been allowed to sink, and it was his
idiosyncratic mix of ideological references with a strong
neo-liberal flavour that would bring salvation. With this
personalisation of power goes the authoritarianism and
aggression which have been amongst the hallmarks of the
presidency, and in this respect the influence of the extreme
right is clear. His manic and at times irascible approach
served to underline his single-minded determination.

But in terms of political programme, the messages he
conveyed often appeared to contradict one other, or at least
were confusing for many. For example, he promoted both
neo-liberalism and a certain degree of protectionism; he
was both against what he viewed as excessive and damag-

ing immigration and in favour of positive discrimination; he was in favour of traditional values and keen to break moulds. The net effect of these heterogeneous and sometimes contradictory signals was to place emphasis on the importance of Sarkozy himself as individual saviour and as he rose to the position of president the sole unifying message was that he as an individual politician was the hero of the time who would offer a path to success for a nation in turmoil, a nation which was (according to Sarkozy) wracked with self-doubt.

Indeed, during the year or so which ran up to the presidential elections of 2007, Sarkozy's analysis of the condition of France, his image as a leader and his electoral programme all became intimately linked. For analysts who have watched France closely for some years, his portrayal of a country in turmoil is somewhat surprising, given the amount of discussion there has been since the mid-1980s of the apparent consensual stability of French political life and the modernisation of the economy, all of which contributed to the notion of the alleged 'end of French exceptionalism' (e.g. Furet et al 1988; Chafer and Godin 2010). But there was indeed fairly widespread perception of crisis. First, many believed there were grave and lasting problems with regard to the economy (tns-sofres 2007). Economic growth in 2006 was at 2 per cent, whereas the average for Eurozone countries was 2.7 per cent. There had been a structural budget deficit every year since 1980 and the level of public debt put France fourth from bottom in the league of indebted countries in Europe, after Italy, Belgium and Germany. Since 2003 (after a decade of surpluses) foreign trade had been going further and further into deficit. Unemployment was at over 8 per cent of the active population according to the government's own figures (compared with a Eurozone average of 7.2 per cent and Organisation for Economic Cooperation and Development (OECD) average of 5.6 per cent) and unemployment amongst under 25-year-olds was over 20 per cent. Many mainstream economists suggested that France had failed to adapt to the increasingly European and globalised economy and that the French must, for example, learn to work harder, like their American counterparts (Le Boucher 2007; Faujas 2007; Ricard 2007).

As far as national politics is concerned, the period since 2002 had been overshadowed by the results of the presidential and parliamentary elections of that year. Most notably, Jean-Marie Le Pen went through to the second round of the presidential elections, because he beat the Socialist Party candidate, Lionel Jospin, in the first round. Voters were therefore obliged in the second round to choose between two candidates whom many either strongly disliked (in the case of Le Pen) or deeply mistrusted (Jacques Chirac), or abstain, and the resulting 82 per cent for Chirac bore no resemblance to his actual level of popularity. Moreover, the level of abstentions was very high in both presidential and parliamentary elections, apparently reflecting a generalised disillusionment with political parties and politicians and therefore with the democratic credibility of elections. The level of support for non-mainstream parties of the left or right in the 2002 presidentials was just over 40 per cent of voters, and 30.6 per cent of all registered voters abstained or spoiled their ballots (Hewlett 2004). There had thus been, since 2002, something of a phony-regime atmosphere in national politics. This was compounded after the May 2005 referendum on the proposed constitution of the European Union seemed to confirm the electorate's disenchantment with national political leaders and their programmes. Both President Chirac and his government were in favour of the constitution, whilst the opposition Socialist Party was deeply divided. The French rejected the proposed constitution with a No vote of nearly 55 per cent. Once again, it seemed that neither Chirac, who incidentally was widely believed to have a career built partly on corrupt activities, nor the parties of government, nor the main opposition party represented voters' wishes.

The final but certainly no less important aspect of perceived crisis in France concerns social problems, especially civil unrest in areas with a high proportion of people from ethnic minorities, high unemployment and poor housing. In October and November 2005 there was sustained and widespread rioting after two young men, Zyed Benna and Bouna Traoré, died in the Eastern Paris suburb Clichy-sous-Bois from electric shocks when they tried to hide from pursuing police in an electricity substation. Prime Minister Dominique de Villepin declared a state of emergency, subsequently approved by parliament and extended for three months, which permitted local authorities to impose curfews, conduct house-to-house searches and ban public gatherings. The situation in underprivileged suburbs of large towns and cities had, it seemed, reached crisis point.

It was in this political, economic and social climate that Sarkozy and his supporters attempted to create the image of an exceptional leader who was capable of solving France's problems. It was indeed precisely in relation to France's deprived suburbs that Sarkozy as Minister for the Interior had made what became nationally and internationally well-known remarks, saying in June 2005 that the Courneuve suburb of Paris should be cleaned out with a *kärcher* (high-pressure industrial cleaning equipment), and calling aberrant suburban youth *racaille*, which is usually translated as 'rabble' or 'scum'. He was indeed blamed by some for the subsequent widespread unrest. At any rate, he was already seen as an exceptionally tough and determined defender of law and order, which remained a key part of his image throughout the election campaigns, with little time for those who attempted to understand deviance or perceived deviance by reference to social deprivation. Although Sarkozy did on occasion dwell on the alleged context of the *kärcher* and *racaille* remarks in order to make them seem less harsh, he was careful never to apologise for them, still less to retract them. This populist gamble, reminiscent of some of Le Pen's barely ambiguous and widely condemned remarks (which he also refused to retract), was a calculated risk which could have backfired on him. But it apparently paid off, at least as far as attracting former Le Pen voters was concerned, as we shall see below.

Sarkozy had more generally gone out of his way to emphasise the importance of law and order. The suburban deprivation and associated unrest for which France is now so well known remained one of the main issues throughout the election campaign, and Sarkozy's promise was to be tough on any further rioting or more minor disturbances. His programme included increased sentences for repeat offenders, including minors, a zero tolerance approach to crime in some areas, similar to parts of the USA, and – a point related to law and order in some voters' eyes – stricter control on immigration, with for the first time a Ministry for Immigration and National Identity. As the campaign proceeded some of Sarkozy's rhetoric and positions became increasingly like Le Pen's, from damning remarks about work-shy cheaters to references to genetic explanation for paedophilia, and a general hardening of language and style. The notion of authority was omnipresent.

Sarkozy's clean-sweep, modernising zeal was expressed more concretely in the core of his neo-liberal-inclined economic programme, designed supposedly to reverse and unblock France's stagnant economic state and be more business-friendly. It would cut taxes drastically, including tax breaks on mortgage payments, and relax the 35-hour week by waiving tax and social security contributions on overtime payments. Trade union powers were to be limited by, for example, introducing a guaranteed 'minimum service' during strikes in the public sector so the country could not be shut down during strikes, and the number of public sector workers would be reduced. Universities would be made more autonomous and therefore more entrepreneurial. All this, Sarkozy argued, would add up to an 'an economic and fiscal shock which will mean that France embarks on the road to growth which at present escapes her' (in Parmentier 2007: 2). His praise of hard work and personal achievement and determination to combat what he perceived as weak political correctness prompted such comments as: 'We must dispense with this culture of permanent excuses which consists of explaining everything and then excusing it' (in Leclerc 2008: 29). Indeed the importance of hard work was another *leitmotif* of the campaign,

informing one of its best-known (and much-ridiculed) slo-
gans: 'Work more to earn more.'

Unlike classic Bonapartist leaders in French history, and
in keeping with trends in economic policy internationally,
Sarkozy's main emphasis regarding economic policy is not
so much one of leading by example from the public sector as
one of arguing for the right of the private sector to make
money and encouraging it to do so (although Sarkozy's
programme was by no means a frontal attack on the state
and the public sector). Again, this approach reflects
Sarkozy's own career and personal inclinations, which
include an unashamed desire to enrich himself and move in
monied circles, and he frequents some of the wealthiest
people in France, a point which I shall explore further
below. Paradoxically, Sarkozy was very much part of the
national politics presided over by Jacques Chirac, with
whom Sarkozy has famously fallen out and criticised. But
this, in a way, reinforced his message that he needed to
be an all-powerful leader in order to resolve France's
problems, not a bit player in what he might see as a rather
feeble, relatively consensual regime. By contrast with
Chirac and Mitterrand before him, Sarkozy implied, he was
prepared to be 'politically incorrect', addressing issues that
Mitterrand and Chirac were said to have been too fright-
ened to address, even taking over from Le Pen in being prepared to 'say out loud what others think but keep to
themselves', as Le Pen himself had put it.

This new approach was confirmed in his first speech after
the presidential election results became known:

> The French people has spoken. It has chosen to break with
> the ideas, the habits and the behaviour of the past. I will
> therefore rehabilitate work, authority, morale and respect.
> I will ensure that the nation and national identity is hon-
> oured once again and I will give back to the French the
> pride of being French, and will banish repentance which is
> a form of self hatred and multiple memories which feed the
> hatred of others. The French people has chosen change. I
> will implement this change because this is what I am asked
> to do by the people and because France is in need of it.
> (Sarkozy 2007e: 4)

Lessons from the past

In order to explain the support which such a maverick presidential candidate received, it is necessary to look in a little more detail at certain aspects of the Chirac presidency. Sarkozy's extreme preoccupation with the question of work reflected a long-standing and strong desire on the part of the centre-right and to some extent the centre-left, as well as the employers' organisation *Mouvement des enterprises de France* (MEDEF) since as long ago as the early 1980s, to reform conditions of work and retirement and what were seen as the general conditions for free enterprise. In particular, the state was deemed in various ways to be supporting workers, the unemployed and retired people too much and the challenge was to shift the balance away from state protection and subsidy and towards private enterprise and enrichment through entrepreneurship. The view of many on the centre-right was that the republican, statist orientation of France was a hindrance to economic growth and fuller employment and that a 'modernisation' of the economy, the labour market and more generally the conditions for doing business was urgently needed, along the lines of Britain and the USA in particular. There was a perception that France was being left behind these and other nations and that the shifting balance of global economic power would make this situation worse.

Part of this tradition was a militant labour movement, albeit small in terms of union membership, and the background to the entire Sarkozy project is one where the right, under Chirac, had attempted reforms to the labour market which had been defeated by strike action, street demonstrations and more broadly public opinion, including in elections, a referendum and numerous opinion polls. This was a period during which Sarkozy was intimately acquainted with the view from inside government, as we have seen.

When Jacques Chirac became president of the republic in May 1995, he entered the Elysée Palace on the understanding that he would use state intervention to renew the 'republican pact' and 'heal social fracture'. But in October 1995, in what became known as the Juppé Plan (after Prime

Minister Alain Juppé) the government attempted to reduce social spending (Levy et al 2008; Hassenteufel 2008; Howell 2008). In particular, it sought to raise the statutory age of retirement, reduce pensions for public sector workers and abolish certain special pension schemes (known as *régimes spéciaux*) in particular in public transport and energy which were seen by the government (and many electors) as far too generous and expensive. The level of spending on social security was in future to be decided by parliament instead of by various more immediately interested parties, including by trade union representatives. There were also proposals for substantial tax increases, including Value Added Tax, which was to rise from 18.6 to 20.6 per cent. There was very little consultation on the bill before it was discussed in parliament and the response both by those who would be immediately affected and among the broader public (who would all be affected by the VAT rise) was enormous. There were widely supported strikes in the public sector for six weeks in winter 1995, which led to the almost complete withdrawal of the bill, leaving only the very unpopular increases in VAT.

In a presidency which, after an already inauspicious start, went on to become characterised by contested and defeated reform proposals, political setbacks came thick and fast as well. The first came when Chirac decided to dissolve parliament and hold elections in spring 1997 in order to consolidate his support in the *Assemblée nationale*. But instead the left won the elections, formed a government with participation from greens and communists and a period of *cohabitation* under President Jacques Chirac lasted from 1997 until 2002, with the socialist Lionel Jospin as prime minister. In the presidential elections of 2002, as we have seen, Chirac was able to renew his presidential mandate, but in the first round of the election he received the lowest ever score for a presidential victor in the history of the Fifth Republic. In the second round, he was competing against the FN leader Jean-Marie Le Pen, which tended to undermine the legitimacy of Chirac's numerically-substantial victory. The final party political blow came in May 2005, when the referendum on the proposed European Union constitution produced a No vote with a substantial and conclusive 54.7 per cent voting against, despite support for the draft constitution from both the centre-right and much of the centre-left. This defeat was interpreted as a strong message of opposition to a pro-free market EU but also as an expression of strong opposition to the president of the republic.

In spring 2006, a second attempt at labour reform was defeated in the street. The proposals on the so-called first employment contract (*Contrat première embauche*, hereafter CPE) were ostensibly designed to reduce the high rate of youth unemployment, which was running at twice the overall national level. Employers and the government argued that firms were not taking on younger, unskilled and inexperienced workers because if they underperformed they were difficult and costly to dismiss. The CPE, then, would allow employers to get rid of workers under the age of twenty-six during their first two years in employment without being obliged to provide either explanation or financial compensation. The protests against the CPE proposals, mainly led by students, were large and powerful. At the height of the protests there were over one million people in the streets and according to opinion polls two-thirds of the French were against the proposed changes (Dupin 2007: 148–9). However, the prime minister not only refused to negotiate with the growing anti-CPE movement but also attempted to force the measure through by using article 49.3 of the constitution which makes a bill a matter of confidence, meaning that in order to defeat the bill there must be a motion of censure against the government, supported by an absolute majority. When the trade unions began to get involved, however, the government saw a familiar pattern emerging and withdrew the bill in its entirety.

This was a situation where the ruling elite — both economic and political — were desperate for change, but governments of the centre-right and indeed centre-left had met with dogged and widespread resistance to neo-liberal reform. It was time to resort to a less conventional approach, not unlike the backing of Margaret Thatcher in Britain in the late 1970s whose essence, as Andrew Gamble (1994) has argued, was a stronger state combined with a freer market. The Sarkozy approach was thus very much one of attempting to draw the lessons of the Chirac era and indeed draw lessons from French history more generally. Large sections of the French population had long been deeply resistant to erosion of what might broadly be described as egalitarian aspects of the French model, many of which had been won on the streets over many years or at least were associated with the revolutionary and republican tradition. Change in the direction of capitalist modernisation in the past had therefore often come via the leadership of maverick autocrats with strong Bonapartist tendencies, and in living memory from de Gaulle.

This approach was thus in large part informed by the desire to introduce neo-liberal reform together with reform regarding law and order and immigration, without being defeated by people on the streets. But by contrast to Britain in the 1970s and 1980s, the approach was not to provoke a head-on collision, as Thatcher had done with the miners in the mid-1980s when the Conservative government had achieved a significant and very clear defeat for the trade union movement. Rather, Sarkozy and his colleagues realised that this was too risky a strategy, and indeed one which was almost bound to fail; instead, despite the highly divisive tone and content of some of his speeches and other utterances, the approach was less obviously confrontational. The title of the president's electoral programme, for example, was *Mon projet. Ensemble, tout devient possible* ('My project. Together, everything becomes possible'), and in the programme he emphasises the importance of social dialogue, as well as the need for profound change (Sarkozy 2007b). Indeed, two days before Sarkozy was sworn in as president he met with leaders of the five largest trade union confederations in what was to be the first of many meetings.

Another major area of political concern was the deprivation and revolt among ethnic minorities and the question of immigration, as we have seen. France had become nationally and internationally infamous for the social deprivation which had become almost synonymous with the suburbs of large towns and cities where many first, second and third generations of immigrants lived. The unrest which had broken out in the suburbs, most strikingly in 2005, was a form of revolt against police harassment, racism and high unemployment, but more generally against the way in which France had failed in particular to offer younger generations of children of immigrants anything like the opportunities so many other French people had. It is significant that in addition to four deaths, hundreds of injured demonstrators and police, thousands of burned cars and nearly 500 arrests, 233 public buildings were either burned down or badly damaged (Levy et al 2008: 4). The other side of the same coin was, of course, the rise of the profoundly racist FN since the mid-1980s and its quasi-electoral triumph of 2002 when Le Pen went into the second round of the presidential elections. Sarkozy presented himself as someone who was able to be tough on the questions of unrest in the suburbs and immigration (the two issues were often conflated) but also willing to go to areas where there had been unrest and discuss issues with local inhabitants. As we will see, one of Sarkozy's major achievements from the point of view of the centre-right was to bring FN voters into his fold at the 2007 elections.

The party, business and media

Alongside the more idiosyncratic aspects of Sarkozy's rise to power and subsequent presidency, there is also the highly successful, conventional party politician, who has skilfully used both the formal political system and the Gaullist party machine in order to further his career. At the age of 28, in 1983, Sarkozy became mayor of one of the most wealthy areas in France, the Parisian suburban town Neuilly-sur-Seine, where he remained mayor until 2002 and where he had a very successful legal practice, specialising in business and family law. He was Minister for the Budget from 1993 to 1995 when Edouard Balladur was

prime minister, served two stints as Minister of the Interior
in governments presided over by Jacques Chirac (2002–04
and 2005–07) and in the meantime had a brief spell as Minister of Finance (April–November 2004). He became leader of
the centre-right UMP in 2004 and oversaw its transformation into a party with a greatly increased membership and a
more activist orientation. Notwithstanding his promises of
rupture if elected in 2007, and constant assertions that the
French needed to move beyond the mixture of lethargy and
crisis that characterised the Chirac era, he was himself very
much part of that era and many changes during that period
bore his imprint.

The UMP was created in 2002 after Chirac's victory in the
presidential elections of that year, and was a coming together
of various, previously disparate centre-right currents; the
model and inspiration for the new UMP was the Spanish People's Party led by former Prime Minister José María Aznar
from 1989, who had united various currents on the right,
including ex-Francoists, liberals and Christian democrats
and in doing this Aznar preached renewal and controlled the
party in a highly personal fashion (Dupin 2007: 184; *Le Monde*
17.11.02). In a similar way, Sarkozy led the transformation of
the UMP after he was elected leader in November 2004 by
85 per cent of the 71,000 members who voted (Knapp and
Sawacki 2008: 46–50). Within two years the membership
had more than doubled to 285,000, which was unusually
high for parties of the French right, although it was now
possible to join the party via the internet. As Andrew Knapp
points out, most new members had joined in order to make
sure Sarkozy would become the UMP's presidential candidate in 2007 and the party was to play a crucial role in the
realisation of Sarkozy's ultimate political ambition.

Neuilly not only offered Sarkozy a wholly dependable
political base but also gave him many contacts in the business world, often made via his legal practice. Many of
France's most successful business people live and/or work
in Neuilly and according to *Le Monde* (13.09.05) and
L'Express (09.01.05) a number of them attended dinner parties organised by the Sarkozy family or were close in other

ways before he became president. These included: the Decaux family, which jointly runs the leading advertising firm JCDecaux; the boss of Oréal, Linsay Owen-Jones; Martin Bouygues, principle shareholder in television channel TF1 (and godfather to the President Sarkozy's son Louis); Philippe Charrier (Proctor and Gamble); Antoine Bernheim (Director General of the Italian insurance group Générali); Dominique Desseigne, head of the Groupe Lucien Barrière which manages casinos and luxury hotels; Michel-Edouard Leclerc, head of the supermarket chain Leclerc; Michel Pébereau (BNP Paribas bank); Patrick Kron, from the industrial group Alstom; Carlos Ghosn (Renault-Nissan); and Gérard Mestrallet who is head of energy company Suez (in Dupin 2007: 146–7).

As Jonah Levy (2005: 192-5) has shown, Sarkozy has long had a close relationship with the employers' organisation MEDEF, of which his older brother Guillaume, a textiles entrepreneur, is a former vice president (from 2004 to 2006). Many of the official policy positions held by MEDEF are close or identical to those of Sarkozy as expressed in his election manifesto: erosion of the 35-hour week which had been introduced by the Socialist government in 2000; reducing employment protection; and bringing levels of taxation down to the European average. MEDEF president Antoine Sellière argued for many years that right-wing governments should be doing more to introduce neo-liberal measures and in August 2004 Sellière said the government of the time (during Chirac's presidency) 'has done nothing for business' and in October the same year 'economic stupidity will not build a future for the country'. Sellière was openly very keen on Sarkozy, calling him the 'Zidane of the economy' (*Ibid.*: 192). As Levy points out, when Sarkozy was in government before running for president he challenged the 35-hour week, he had run-ins with Chirac over budgetary policy, including defence spending and employment minister Jean-Louis Borloo's social cohesion plan, and MEDEF pushed government to move in a neo-liberal direction, such as reform of wealth tax (opposed by Chirac, but he did have to accept some changes) and abolition of the 35-hour week.

It was important that, for the first time for many years, big business and smaller businesses alike were united behind Sarkozy; the newspaper *Le Monde* quotes the historian Jean Garrigues in 2005 as saying that Sarkozy

> seems to be the only politician to have conquered the confidence of bosses of the small and medium-sized businesses since Raymond Poincaré in 1926 and Antoine Pinay in 1951, by creating the image of someone with determination, who is prepared to implement radical reforms and to break with a political class seen as incapable of understanding economic problems. (In Dupin 2007: 147).

It seemed that, oddball though he was, Sarkozy was able for the first time to count on the support of a united business community; as Dupin (2007: 148) points out, they had been divided between presidential candidates Barre and Chirac in 1988, and Balladur and Chirac in 2005, but they were now united in a desire to see a tough-minded member of their own kind in office who was at last prepared to drive through necessary reforms after so many years of hesitation, false starts and backing down on the part of other politicians. Indeed, MEDEF's collective manifesto published in 2007 even had a distinctly Sarkozyist (and by the same token anti-Chirac) title, namely *Un besoin d'agir* ('A need to act') (MEDEF 2007).

Just as importantly, Sarkozy is not a graduate of the elite civil service college, the ENA, nor any other *grande école* for that matter, which so many high level right-wing politicians since the Second World War have been. Georges Pompidou (who was president from 1969 to 1974) was a graduate of ENA, Valéry Giscard d'Estaing (1974–81) attended both ENA and *Ecole polytechnique*, and Jacques Chirac (1995–2007) studied both at ENA and *Sciences Po*. Instead of relying primarily on administrative elites, then, which had been so important to parliamentary and presidential politics for so many years, but who were often perceived not to understand the world of business, Sarkozy relied greatly on the business elite. This became even clearer when the composition of the guest list at expensive Parisian restaurant Fouquet's on the night of the presidential electoral victory was made public. By way of election victory celebration, expression of gratitude for support over previous months and years, and an indication of the continued support he was anticipating over the years to come, Sarkozy invited some of the best-placed business people in France and abroad, collectively representing colossal wealth. The list (in Plenel 2010: 22–3) speaks volumes as to the elite support base for the president and was made up of fifty-five people, including some of the most powerful in business, politics, show business and the media. They included: Mathilde Agostinelli, Director of Communication, Prada France; Bernard Arnault, chair and CEO of the luxury goods conglomerate LVMH and France's richest individual; Nicolas Bavarez, writer and journalist at the right-leaning news magazine *Le Point*, who believes France has been allowed to decline in relation to other industrialised countries; Nicolas Beytout, editor of right-leaning newspaper *Le Figaro*; Vincent Bolloré, president of Havas, sixth largest media group in the world; Martin Bouygues, principle shareholder in television channel TF1 (as mentioned above); Serge Dassault, head of both aeronautics group Dassault, which is majority shareholder in Socpresse, and which owns newspapers *Le Figaro* and *L'Express* (ranked 56th in the world's richest people); Jean-Claude Decaux, Director General of JCDecaux (also mentioned above); Albert Frère, the richest person in Belgium who made his fortune largely in the steel industry; and Guillaume Sarkozy, brother of Nicolas and former vice president of the employers' organisation MEDEF. Once again, the Fouquet's meal, immediately followed by Sarkozy's brief holiday on Bolloré's yacht, was not only symbolic — that is a reflection — of the support he received but also confirmed that the commercial elite had triumphed over the administrative elite.

Sarkozy was also extremely well-placed to influence the media, and went out of his way to do so. Mamère and Farbiaz (2009: 9) argue convincingly that Sarkozy represents the most extreme example since 1958 of the fusion of politics, money and the media. In a way that was unprecedented in modern French politics, he had close relationships — in the personal, business and political senses — with media bosses, owners and reporters, not to mention television and film stars. Indeed, his own life became increasingly similar to that of television, film or rock star, and his affair and subsequent marriage to successful singer and former model Carla Bruni served only to reinforce this image. The reality show nature of his private and political life in the months after his election and intense media interest in every aspect of his life served to reinforce the personalised nature of his power and the sense that he, in voluntarist fashion could apparently achieve exactly what he wanted (e.g. Duhamel 2009: 73). Artufel and Duroux (2006) describe how in the year or two before the election of 2007 the Sarkozy machine carefully controlled relations with the media, feeding almost endless sound bites and eye-catching headlines, creating photo opportunities — such as Sarkozy in running shorts, on holiday and with his children — and generally courting sympathetic journalists.

Opposition parties

If, as argued above, Sarkozy's success was in large part due to a carefully constructed brand of authoritarian populism which struck a chord in the particular political, economic and social circumstances of the time, his success was also of course the result of other parties' and other candidates' failures. Most importantly, given the bi-polar logic of presidential elections in France, where in the second round there are only two candidates, we must look at the Socialist Party and its candidate, Ségolène Royal.

Since the death in 1996 of François Mitterrand, the historic re-builder of the Socialist Party and president for fourteen years (1981–95), the party has struggled to find either strategy or leader able to offer lasting success. Although during its many years in government since 1981 the PS has — at least since 1983 — been a highly pragmatic party of compromise, the positions of its various factions vying for control are still influenced by a rather notional dilemma between more traditional re-distributional socialism on the one hand and what might be described as post-socialist 're-alism' on the other. Many within the party are now calling for a 'social-democratisation' of the PS, by which they mean changes to make the PS more like the British Labour Party or the German *Sozialdemokratische partei Deutschlands* (SPD); in government the PS already behaves only a step or two to the left of what used to be called Third Way politics, but its rhetoric – in particular when out of national office – tends to be more to the left. Profound dilemmas over ideology, strategy and leadership have thus been part of the party's public profile for over a decade and the dominant individuals in the leadership were far from united behind Ségolène Royal as presidential candidate. Disagreements abounded between the major figures including Royal, François Hollande, Dominique Strauss-Kahn (who is a foremost advocate of a Blairised PS), and Laurent Fabius.

The socialist current in France certainly has a problem regarding both sociology and tactics. It re-emerged as a party of government during the 1970s by means of an alliance with the then strong Communist Party, which meant that working class voters who tended to vote communist were attracted to the left camp more generally, leading eventually to Mitterrand's victory in the presidential elections in 1981. Today, with the *Parti communist français* (PCF) attracting so few votes, such an alliance is of little use, and increasing numbers of blue-collar workers have over the past few decades turned to the FN as a party of protest against the mainstream. In order to win national elections, the PS, like any party, needs to capture both blue- and white-collar salaried workers in large numbers, which is something that Sarkozy understood well; while he talked of neo-liberal *rupture* in economic policy he also spoke, for example, of the necessary protective action of the state, and of Europe protecting France from the ravages of globalisation. His discourse on law and order also had broad appeal.

This historical and structural problem for the PS meant that after the first round of the presidential election an alliance with the centre was necessary if Royal was to have any chance of winning. Between the two rounds, then, Royal (to the dismay of some other PS leaders) attempted to elicit clear, public support from *Union pour la démocratie Française* (UDF) centre-right candidate François Bayrou, whose help would have been arithmetically particularly useful given that he polled 18.6 per cent in the first round. She even offered ministerial positions to the UDF in return for their support, but Bayrou was not convinced. Royal could count on the support of the far left, Greens and Communists, but not from the UDF, and this did not add up to a Sarkozy-beating majority. (The UDF became *Mouvement démocrate*, usually known as MODEM, between the presidential elections and the parliamentary elections of 2007.)

Certainly, Royal broke the PS mould to the extent that she was not an entrenched and long-running participant in the major power struggles within the party, or at least not as much as other key figures. Neither was she a man in a dark suit. Her views were also eclectic and sometimes idiosyncratic, rather than rehearsing well-worn themes. She had quickly won a great deal of support for her nomination within the party, easily beating the other two contenders for presidential candidate nomination, Dominique Strauss-Kahn and Laurent Fabius. In terms of campaigning and policies, Royal's emphasis on the experience of ordinary people was on the whole popular and she spoke often of family values, discipline, authority and the protection of children. But her programme was perceived by many as being vague and short on detail, with far less talk or in-depth knowledge of international relations or economic policy than might be expected from a presidential candidate.

Regarding the far left, compared with the 2002 presidential elections, when parties to the left of the Socialists and Communists received 10 per cent of the vote, the far left performed badly in 2007. This is perhaps surprising, given the degree of disillusionment with mainstream politicians, together with high levels of public protest over issues such as proposed weakened employment protection and pay for younger employees, and the large No vote at the referendum over the European constitution in May 2005. However, it seems voters were fearful that if they voted far left in the first round there would be a repeat of the 2002 elections, when the PS candidate Lionel Jospin failed to go through to the second round and the French were presented with a choice between the right and the extreme right. Perhaps more importantly, there was no agreement on the far left regarding a single candidate, apparently confirming the view that it is deeply factionalised and more concerned with in-fighting over small points of difference than with real change. Dominique Voynet, for the Greens, also did very badly, similarly reflecting years of in-fighting between different ecologist parties, factions and individuals.

We will return to the plight of the FN below. Suffice it to say here that Le Pen and his party were severely damaged in 2007 by Sarkozy deliberately attempting to attract former FN voters to his own camp.

Interpreting the 2007 election results

Returning to the 2007 election results (Appendices 1–4), we see that in the first round of the presidential elections abstention was particularly low for the Fifth Republic, especially in recent years, reinforcing Sarkozy's claim to legitimacy as the clear front-runner, with nearly two million more votes than Royal. Sarkozy's vote was the highest ever in the Fifth Republic in terms of actual votes cast, but not amongst the highest in terms of proportion of votes cast. It was, however, immediately clear that Sarkozy's aggressively right- and in parts extreme-right-oriented campaign and programme had won over many voters, leaving Le Pen with only 10.5 per cent of the total, compared with 16.9 per cent in 2002. Many voters broke with the tradition of 'voting with their hearts' in the first round and 'with their heads' in the second round, and voted with their heads—for parties of government—from the beginning. This was in part because of the fiasco of the 2002 presidential elections and helps explain, as argued above, the low vote for the smaller parties of the left.

In the second round of the presidential elections, the rate of abstention was lower than in any presidential election since 1965, the year of the first presidential election by universal suffrage in the Fifth Republic. Sarkozy won with nearly 19 million votes—over two million more than Royal—or 53.1 per cent of the total. In terms of second rounds which were left-right run-offs, Sarkozy was approaching the record percentage score of de Gaulle, who received 54.5 percent in 1965 against Mitterrand. In terms of actual votes cast, Sarkozy won 3.2 million more than Chirac in 1995, and 2.2 million more than Mitterrand in 1988, who at that time held the record number of votes in the Fifth Republic. Again, the very high rate of participation reinforced Sarkozy's claim to legitimacy and was interpreted as a mandate for personalised power.

A brief description of Sarkozy's behaviour between presidential and parliamentary elections is important for an understanding of what followed. It was clear that he would rule in a controlling and centralised fashion, a desire facilitated by reducing the number of ministers by half; this smaller, more tightly-controlled government was led by Sarkozy loyalist and former Minister of Social Affairs, Work and Solidarity (2002–04), François Fillon, and a Minister for Immigration and National Identity (close ally Brice Hortefeux) was appointed. On the one hand, Sarkozy confirmed that the programme of reforms would take place very fast, starting with an extraordinary summer parliamentary session. Not long after victory, the news headlines described how Sarkozy had appointed a faithful ally, Frédéric Péchenard, as Director General of Police which, as Piotr Smolar commented in *Le Monde*, 'translates the will of the Elysée Palace to implement scrupulously its reform projects as far as law and order are concerned' (Smolar 2007: 1). Meanwhile, Laurent Solly, his deputy campaign director, became head of the television channel TF1.

On the other hand, in characteristically maverick fashion, Sarkozy pursued what was described as *ouverture* (literally 'opening'), which meant, notably, appointing PS member, *Médecins sans frontières* founder and pro-American Bernard Kouchner as Foreign Minister, examined in more detail in Chapter Four. Such *ouverture* was not just populist *largesse*, however, but was designed also to neutralise somewhat the Socialist Party, making it seem as if the PS was already represented in government and did not need a large number of votes in the parliamentary elections.

The first round of the parliamentary elections saw a record high level of abstentions, at 39.6 per cent. This seemed to indicate not only that voters were beginning to suffer from voting fatigue, but also to confirm that that presidential elections were seen as the more important national elections of the Fifth Republic, with parliamentary elections simply confirming the result of the presidentials. The results certainly did confirm Sarkozy and the UMP as far more popular than Royal and the PS; the UMP won 45.2 per cent of the vote (an exceptionally high level for any party in the Fifth Republic) and the PS 27.7 per cent. The decline of the FN was confirmed with its 4.3 per cent in the first round, compared with 11.4 per cent in 2002.

At the second round of the parliamentary elections, however, the UMP failed to gain the overwhelming result they anticipated as they became victims, it seems, of Sarkozy and his followers' over-confidence. In fact voters delivered what *Le Monde* (19.06.07) described in its front page headline as 'a warning intended for Sarkozy'. The electorate was apparently strongly affected by discussions of the possible five percentage-point increase in VAT, *TVA sociale*. This was planned in order to pay for reductions in social security contributions for employers, thus reducing labour costs and moving taxation further onto consumption. The promised landslide thus failed to materialise, although the UMP did achieve an absolute majority of seats in the National Assembly. One particularly serious blow for the new government was the defeat of the second most important minister and former Prime Minister Alain Juppé, who resigned from his post after losing his seat in the Gironde. All this notwithstanding, Prime Minister Fillon declared that the parliamentary elections 'validate a plan to modernise France in a resolute fashion' and reminded the public that his government would continue to work on the promised new laws in work, employment, purchasing power, security, modernisation of universities, assuring a minimum service during strikes, and on immigration (Fottorino 2007).

Looking back at the breakdown by age and social class of Sarkozy and Royal's electorates in the second round of the presidential elections, it seems that Sarkozy's populist image and assurances that he represented all French people did strike a certain chord. Appendix 4 shows this broad spread over different age groups and different social groups and, although there is particular support from farmers and the self-employed, the Sarkozy electorate is not unlike de Gaulle's and that of the populist and hard-right-inclined Gaullist *Rassemblement du peuple français* (RPF) in its heyday in the late 1940s and early 1950s.

The extreme right

I hope to have shown that there are clear Bonapartist characteristics in the way in which Sarkozy constructed a particular image and managed to persuade a broad electorate to support him. I have dwelt long on Sarkozy as an individual politician because one of the principal characteristics of Bonapartism is of course the promotion of one person whom their supporters argue is exceptionally suited to leading the nation in what are seen as unusual circumstances. This does not signify the absence of political and economic agenda. Quite the contrary. As we have seen, Sarkozy came to power with a far-reaching, largely neo-liberal agenda, overlaid with patriotism, emphasis on law and order, together with populist nods towards a fairer lot for the ordinary working person, including acknowledgement of the need for state protection.

It should also be said that there are, in René Rémond's (1982) terms and highly schematically, both counter-revolutionary and Orleanist — that is extreme right and liberal-right — tendencies in Sarkozy's recipe for success, although these are less pronounced. Sarkozy was successful in undermining the electorate of the FN in both presidential and parliamentary elections, which was arithmetically a key element in his success. Sarkozy and the UMP were attempting to do — albeit far more rapidly — to the FN what Mitterrand had done to the PCF; just as in the early 1970s Mitterrand stated publically that, in his view, out of five million Communist voters three million should be voting Socialist, during the 2007 election campaign Sarkozy declared:

> Yes, I want to attract Le Pen voters. Who could blame me for bringing these people back into the republican fold? I will even go and find them one by one — I don't mind that at all. The Front national made progress and that means we on the right did not do our job properly. (In Fourquet 2007: 1)

In a highly revealing article by Jérôme Fourquet, we see that in the areas where Le Pen was strong in 2002, Sarkozy made real gains in 2007 over candidates of the mainstream right in 2002. The increases were particularly large in the Mediterranean departments and Sarkozy's highest score anywhere in France was in the normally FN-sympathetic Alpes-Maritimes, with 43.6 per cent of votes. In a large-scale survey, Fourquet found that Sarkozy's tough reaction to clashes between youths and police at the Gare du Nord in Paris in March 2007 encouraged former Le Pen voters to vote Sarkozy instead of Le Pen, as did Sarkozy's more general positions on what might broadly be termed delinquency. Given the choice between various different aspects of his policies, they were particularly impressed by the president-in-waiting's views on law and order: Fourquet notes that a quarter of what he describes as the most faithful, 'hard core' FN supporters had even more faith in Sarkozy's views on the key theme of *sécurité* than in Le Pen's. (Fourquet 2007: 5).

Sarkozy has also, of course, certain characteristics of the Orleanist liberal-right, which arguably largely characterised the politics of Giscard d'Estaing in particular and also, in part at least, François Bayrou. But there was a real shift of emphasis, of which Sarkozy himself is both entirely aware and proud, claiming that 'if I had followed in the footsteps of my predecessors, we would have lost everything' (in Ridet 2007: 23).

A final point to be made here is that Bonapartism is and always has been inherently unstable, because it is built upon flimsy bases. It is volatile and particularly vulnerable to the changes in the whims of voters, many of whom were in April, May and June 2007 persuaded more by image than by the longer-term practical logic of the proposed reforms. We should not forget that many people made up their minds which way to vote right at the last minute, and that all mainstream politicians were widely unpopular well into the election campaign. Moreover, the fragility of politics infused with Bonapartist tendencies means that it is prone to successful challenge by people on the street, and whatever Sarkozy might preach, the predilection for demonstration and protest in France is not a thing of the past.

May 1968

To conclude this examination of the rise of Sarkozy to the position of president of the republic, I will look at the views he expressed on the student and worker uprising of May 1968, which are highly revealing. There were many references to the Events of May in the weeks and months leading up to the May 2007 elections, and on 17 April in a speech in Metz, for example, Sarkozy declared:

> May 1968 was all about that. Down with authority. That is the programme of May 1968: ... the child obeying its parent is finished; the power of the police is finished; politeness, courtesy, respect for traditional values is finished ... But I want to have done with the legacy of May 1968. (Sarkozy 2007c)

Sarkozy devoted a large part of the last major public speech of his presidential campaign to his views on the legacy of the events, a speech delivered on 29 April 2007 at the *Palais d'Omnisports* in Bercy, Paris (Sarkozy 2007d). It is worth quoting from and analysing the speech in some detail, as it expresses something of the essence of his approach to gaining the highest political office in the land. First, he sets the scene by carefully putting the election in the context in which he wishes it to be seen, namely one of profound crisis:

No, this was not a campaign like other campaigns.

This was a campaign which grappled with a moral crisis, with a crisis of identity such as France has perhaps never seen before in her entire history, except perhaps in the time of Joan of Arc and the Treaty of Troyes, when national conscience was so fragile …

No, this campaign was not a campaign like others. This campaign was perhaps the most morally-demanding of all campaigns.

This campaign required more authenticity, more sincerity, more truth than all other campaigns because the problem which was posed was deeper, more serious, more heavy with consequences.

He goes on to list a number of ordinary people he has gone to see because they are victims of the 'moral crisis', in the form for example of attacks by gangs, commenting that 'I went to meet the people, this people in the name of whom everyone claims to speak, to whom no-one truly speaks, and for whom no-one really wants to do anything.' He adds: 'It is for them that I wish to speak. I want to be their mouthpiece' and he argues in favour of a return of the political, 'the need for politics to become once more the expression of a will'. He continues:

But politics is coming back. It is coming back the world over. The fall of the Berlin Wall seemed to announce the end of History and the dilution of politics into the market. Eighteen years later everyone knows that History is not over, that History is still tragic and that politics cannot disappear, because people today feel a need for politics, a desire for politics that one has rarely seen since the end of the Second World War.

Arguing that the return of politics must mean the return of morality in politics, Sarkozy declares that the legacy of May 1968 is precisely the antithesis of morality:

The word 'moral' does not frighten me. After May 1968 we could no longer speak of morality. It was a word that had disappeared from the political vocabulary. For the first time for decades, morality has been [in 2007] at the heart of a presidential campaign.

Then he declares that the spirit of May 1968 is at the source of the downhill slide which French society has experienced:

> May 1968 had imposed on us an intellectual and moral relativity. Those who defended May 1968 had imposed the idea that everything was of equal value, that there was no difference between good and evil, between true and false, between beautiful and ugly.
>
> They wanted us to believe that the pupil was on a par with the teacher, that school marks were wrong because they traumatised the bad pupils, that there should not be differentiation.
>
> They wanted us to believe that the victim counted less than the delinquent.
>
> They wanted us to believe that there could be no hierarchy between values.
>
> They proclaimed that everything was permitted, that authority was finished, that good manners were finished, that respect was finished, that there was no longer anything great, or sacred, nothing admirable, no more rules, no more norms, no more prohibitions.

May 1968 at this point becomes the root cause of all wrong, including bad schooling (where schools no longer convey a 'common culture') and cynicism in politics.

The speech is thus highly revealing in its detail of how Sarkozy wishes to present himself as populist, autocratic saviour. He concentrates on morality and traditional values in order to attract both older and extreme right voters. But beyond that, it is significant that he should choose to target the events of May in such a clear and lengthy way. Beyond the 'moral decline' he claims May 1968 represents, there is a more important issue — a barely coded message for the capitalist class — which this line of argument represents: the events of May are the prime example in post-war Western Europe of the power of ordinary people taking to the streets, of collective action, with not only the student uprising, but also the three-and-a-half-week-long general strike, when factories were occupied and many workers were in highly radical frame of mind. The spectre of May 1968 has haunted numerous attempts at neo-liberal reform since then, including Chirac's attempts in 1995 and 2006. In ideological terms, to attack moral decline was important in consolidating the right and particularly far right electorate which was crucial to Sarkozy's success, but in politico-economic terms he wished to send the message that he was willing to drive through a neo-liberal agenda in a way no previous government had been able to do.

However, the deeply populist aspect of the message becomes clearer when Sarkozy declares, most extraordinarily and with a breath-taking display of mental gymnastics, that the decline of traditional, respectable capitalism — and this speech was of course made well before the beginning of the financial crisis — has the same roots:

> Look how the cult of money, short-term profit, speculation and the excesses of finance capitalism have been borne by the values of May 1968.

> Look how the challenging of all ethical points of reference and of moral values has contributed towards weakening the morality of capitalism, how it prepared the ground for unscrupulous and ethics-free capitalism with its golden handshakes, luxurious retirements and thuggish bosses, how it led to the triumph of the predator over the entrepreneur, the speculator over the worker.

Having described the left as not caring for ordinary people any longer and claiming to do so far more himself, he returns to and concludes (barring a brief hommage to de Gaulle) with a key theme: 'I want to rehabilitate work. I want to give the prime place in society back to the worker.'

To summarise and interpret, I have already noted that Sarkozy is firstly attempting to appeal to both the centre-right and the extreme right (especially in the comments on capitalist greed). Second, May 1968 is associated with intellectuals and with public sector workers and in particular with university lecturers and teachers; these are anyway largely a lost cause in right-wing electoral terms and are a prime target of the counter-revolution that Sarkozy is spearheading. Next, references to May 1968 are also references to more recent revolts and movements associated with the left, which Sarkozy is prepared for. At a more general level, Sarkozy's obsession with May 1968 and his wish to bury it once and for all is an expression of a bid to be leader of a counter-revolution against what 1968 stood for, so a counter-revolution in terms of morality, nationalism, ideology, the economy, industrial relations, foreign relations, and the individual versus the collective.

Chapter Four

The Challenge of the Highest Office

Times are certainly hard, but I will help you in the work that
needs to be done. Be courageous. I will protect you.

From a speech by Sarkozy on 29 November 2007
on the economic crisis, broadcast on TF1 and France 2
(quoted in Hauser 2008: 29)

In previous chapters I have argued that Sarkozy managed
to achieve high office because the particular socio-economic
and political conditions favoured an individual who was
undoubtedly a maverick, despite also being part of the
mainstream right. Somewhat exceptional circumstances
prompted recourse to an apparently mould-breaking individual preaching politics which would enable a fresh start.
By those voters more naturally on the right, Sarkozy was
seen as offering a particular 'modernising' solution to a
series of ongoing problems, some of them more characteristic of France than many other advanced industrial countries
such as a large public sector and certain perceived constraints on business. For some who were not so conventionally or predictably supporters of the right, Sarkozy seemed
to offer sufficient appeal to be worth backing, at least in the
absence of a credible left alternative, because his approach
included elements of protest against the status quo, or at
least movement as opposed to stasis. This was also appeal-
ing to some on the extreme right, who played an important
part in his election victory. I placed emphasis on what might
be termed 'extraordinary' approaches to the construction of

the Sarkozy myth, dwelling on the image of Sarkozy as autocrat and saviour, determined to save France from the supposedly perilous situation it was in. But I also examined the background and some of the tactics used by Sarkozy to arrive in a position of high office which might be regarded as more conventional and more expected from a conservative politician. This involved working closely with traditional business interests and conservative party political structures and individuals, a strategy which was successful not only in terms of securing the presidency, but also achieving substantial victory over his opponents on the left and indeed on the old-guard right as well, not to mention the FN.

In this chapter, I examine the approach of Sarkozy and his government to ruling the country once he became president of the republic. As soon as he was elected, he set about reforming France with what can only be described as manic zeal, implementing a bewildering array of diverse — and in some cases almost incomprehensible — changes. This is a strategy which will need some explanation in the first section of the chapter. Through the blizzard of new laws, one discernable thread which ran through many was a desire to introduce what could broadly be described as neo-liberal reform, designed to make France's economy still more conducive to entrepreneurial activity than it had been before and with less intervention by the state. This will form the next point of focus. I then examine ways in which Sarkozy reinforced the already powerful position of president, both in terms of formal regulations — the constitution of the Fifth Republic — and in terms of style, with a great deal of help from the media. Finally, I examine the way in which the regime fared in local elections and more generally in terms of popularity among the general public, which was, to say the least, mixed.

Three, related points are worth making before embarking on a more detailed analysis of Sarkozy in power. First, the economic crisis meant that the conditions in which the Sarkozy regime was operating were significantly different from those which had been predicted and this of course needs exploring. Second, although there was a logic to the way in which he went about governing, once in power there was also a fairly pragmatic — and at times opportunist — approach to reforms and positions, rather than following a strict blueprint. Finally, the significant — and at least described by the government as far-reaching — changes were mainly made in the first eighteenth months of the presidential term, in part because of the desire to act very fast, and in part because the recession began in earnest in mid- to late 2008 and, among other things, contributed to increased unemployment and increased public sector deficit, both of which had the effect of creating a climate which made labour, economic and welfare reforms more difficult to achieve.

Tactics of the Sarkozy regime

I have argued that an important reason for the support from the UMP and the business community for Sarkozy as presidential candidate was the series of failures to introduce new legislation under Chirac, particularly in the domain of work and labour relations. The tactics employed by Sarkozy in order to avoid the defeats and failures the right had experienced over the previous twelve years can be divided into four main categories. The first was to recruit to positions in government or as government advisors members of the mainstream left and others who were quite clearly not part of the mainstream right. The most high profile member of his first government who was formerly a member of the PS was *Médecins sans frontières* founder and pro-American Bernard Kouchner, who had been Minister for Health in Socialist governments, UN Special Representative in Kosovo and had supported the invasion of Iraq in 2003, albeit on humanitarian, anti-Saddam Hussein grounds. Kouchner had backed Ségolène Royal in the 2007 presidential election campaign but was made foreign minister immediately after Sarkozy became president, which prompted Kouchner's expulsion from the PS. The second most important government nomination from the left was Eric Besson, who had been National Secretary of the PS until February 2007. After holding a more junior post from May 2007 Besson became Minister for Immigration, Integration, National Identity and Development Solidarity in January 2009 and in the same month he became assistant general secretary of the UMP. The shift from left to right was itself a coup for Sarkozy, and Besson occupying such a key — and confusingly-titled, typically-Sarkozyist — ministry in which he pursued a decidedly hard line, was another. Other individuals formerly from the left included former PS associate Jean-Pierre Jouyet as Junior Minister for Europe and Jean-Marie Bockel as Junior Minister for *Francophonie*. Bockel, a self-confessed Blairite in the PS, set up *Gauche moderne* in 2007, which he claimed was both centre-left and pro-Sarkozy. Moreover, François Mitterrand's nephew Frédéric Mitterrand was made Minister for Culture in June 2009, and although he had not been a member of the PS, to appoint a close relative of the iconic Socialist leader was intended as a strong message that Sarkozy was not simply a conventional, conservative politician.

Sarkozy also appointed the high-profile former Socialist culture minister and Minister for Education Jack Lang as special envoy to both Cuba and North Korea in late 2009 and former Socialist Prime Minister Michel Rocard advised on reform programmes in various domains, including education and carbon tax. A host of other well-known Socialists acted as advisors in one capacity or another, including François Mitterrand's former special advisor Jacques Attali, who led a Commission for Economic Growth, and Michel Charasse who is on the Constitutional Council. The former Socialist Finance Minister Dominique Strauss-Kahn was nominated by the French government and became head of the International Monetary Fund in September 2007, but he remains in the PS.

Just as importantly, Sarkozy also nominated to important positions two high profile leaders of national pressure groups which were non-party political but were generally associated with the left. As we have seen, Martin Hirsch, former president of homeless charity Emmaüs France, was

High Commissioner for Poverty Eradication from 2007 to 2010 (leaving government after the regional elections). Fadela Amara, former head of the well-known and successful feminist group NPNS became Junior Minister for Urban Regeneration in June 2007, although she was still a municipal councillor for the PS at the time. Moreover, in a country where ethnic minorities and women were greatly underrepresented in government, the appointment of Amara, Rachida Dati (as Justice Minister, before resigning and becoming an MEP in 2009) and Rama Yade (as Junior Minister for Human Rights, becoming Secretary of State for Sport in June 2009, widely seen as demotion for not running for membership of the European Parliament), all women from ethnic minorities, seemed to send a decidedly innovative message in itself. There were far more women in important governmental positions than had been seen for many years and these included Christine Lagarde as Minister of Economic Affairs, Industry and Employment; Michèle Alliot-Marie as Minister of the Interior; and Roselyne Bachelot-Narquin as Minister of Health.

Although government remained greatly dominated by long-term members of the UMP and the appointment of others had little impact on the overall direction in which it was moving, there is no doubt that these appointments reflecting *ouverture* did demoralise and weaken both parliamentary and extra-parliamentary opposition to Sarkozy. In particular, it reinforced the image of the PS as a party where talented individuals would abandon the socialists in favour of a political movement which was having substantial influence on the direction the country was travelling, as opposed to a highly divided and possibly spent force, as the PS was often described. More generally, it served to reinforce Sarkozy's message that he wished to put the nation first and have done with sectarian interests and the Kouchner and Besson appointments were particularly important as symbols of how Sarkozy appeared to blur the boundaries between right and left, in an ostensible move to rise above partisan divisions. These are highly Bonapartist characteristics. *Ouverture* also, however, divided the right and there was a certain amount of back-pedalling on this tactic after the disastrous results for the UMP in the regional elections in 2010.

The strategy of appointing high profile members of activist groups to government positions also tends to bypass grass roots activism and send the message that it is well-placed individuals that make a difference, not collective action. It undermines the work of grass roots organisations whose leaders have been persuaded to join the government, sending the message that rank and file activism is not necessary if there is direct access to — and participation in — government. Marcos Ancelovi (2008: 90) describes how NPNS was badly affected by Amara taking a post in the Fillon government, particularly as she was answerable to Minister of Housing and Urban Development Christine Boutin, whose reputation is both solidly right-wing and anti-abortion. Indeed, more than twenty local committees of NPNS closed down in the months following Amara's appointment and many cooperated in forming a new organisation called *Les insoumis-es* (literally: the un-submissives) as a direct response to Amara's apparent support for Sarkozy's policies.

What united the disparate members of the government, then, was their loyalty to Sarkozy and his very particular and personal approach to governing the country, rather than loyalty to a detailed political programme. Thus having disparate people as ministers reinforces Sarkozy's position as supreme leader. The logic of this was also to weaken, destabilise, disorient and disarm the opposition and to some extent to disorient his own side. It also, of course, attracts a great deal of media attention.

The second major tactic employed by Sarkozy was that in terms of policy formulation he concentrated on some domains and issues which were traditionally more associated with the left than with the right, including work, ecology and education, all areas to which we will return below. We have already seen how Sarkozy went out of his way to mix ideological references, invoking major historical figures from the left, including Léon Blum, Jean Jaurès and even the Italian Communist leader and intellectual, Antonio Gramsci. We have also seen how in the presidential campaign he sought to attract working class voters by promising a higher standard of living, *rupture* with what went before and state intervention where necessary for the most vulnerable. In December 2006 he had made a speech where he spoke to 'the France which is suffering', in other words those who were unemployed, underpaid, or living in other precarious conditions, promising state protection for the most needy (Sarkozy 2006). Two areas of reform illustrate the blurring of ideological boundaries in this way. The first is the new state-provided *Revenu de solidarité active* (RSA), a state benefit which was introduced in June 2009 to replace the *Revenu minimum d'insertion* (RMI) and lone parent allowance, and which is mainly intended to top up lower (typically part-time) salaries in order to get people back into work. Superficially, the RSA, which includes the important, left-associated word 'solidarity' in its name, is a win-win new measure. The government website insists that it: 'encourages people to work; boosts low incomes earned from employment; provides individual support for recipients; [and] simplifies the system of welfare benefits' (www.rsa.gouv.fr/What-is-rSa,606.html). Taken as a whole, however, the RSA also tends to encourage the casualisation of work on employers' terms and keep the wage bill down, rather than encouraging the creation of full-time, permanent jobs with a proper career structure.

Turning now to ecology, Sarkozy was insistent that the new government should organise a consultation process which was described as a Grenelle of the Environment . The word *grenelle* is significant and is a reference to the tripartite talks between government, employers and trade unions at the employers' organisation headquarters in rue de Grenelle, Paris, at the end of May 1968. These talks effectively brought the vast workers' protest movement to an end but with relatively few long-term gains for the labour movement. More concretely, the Grenelle of the Environment was designed to poach on the territory not only of the left but even more obviously the Greens, who have a substantial following in France. Sarkozy and the Ecology

Minister Jean-Louis Borloo launched the large and high-profile consultation process which brought together five different sets of interests, namely: pressure groups; the national state; local authorities; employers' organisations; and trade unions (Szarka 2009: 416). There were 273 policy proposals which came out of this process and there was a framework law passed in 2008. The proposals were indeed substantial and in particular planned a 75 per cent reduction in greenhouse gases by 2050, an ambitious goal which appeared to send a clear message of commitment to certain ecological issues and which contrasted with France's previously fairly weak environmental policies. Sarkozy went on to put together the European Union 'climate energy package' in late 2008 during the French presidency of the EU, which added legitimacy to the national environmental process. However, after the regional elections of March 2010 the planned carbon tax—which would have been broadly applicable and would have reigned in large, polluting industries to some extent (despite many exemptions) and had been hailed by Sarkozy as a vital weapon in the fight against global warming—was dropped in a bid to win back greater support from the traditional right and the business community (*Le Point* 25.03.10: 50).

Joseph Szarka (2009: 407–8) argues that here again the intention was in part to demonstrate a preoccupation with issues of national concern rather than narrow, 'sectarian' preoccupations which would have been more likely to encourage and enable opposition in various forms. This, he argues, is an example of what is sometimes described as syncretism, or 'the incomplete fusion of divergent schools of thought'. Szarka also mentions 'triangulation' which means (quoting Grunberg and Haegel 2007: 111) that 'in order to oppose an adversary, the best solution is not to delegitimise the theses that he takes on, but on the contrary to re-appropriate them'. Thus

> [t]hemes associated with political rivals are reinterpreted and exploited in terms that are compelling both for a candidate's core electorate and for swing voters from other parties. Sarkozy's mastery of the discourse of 'triangulation'

> during the presidential campaign enabled him to extend
> his electoral reach, breaking into the political space of the
> far right whilst rehearsing the concerns of the left. It pro-
> vides a key illustration of his syncretic strategies. (Szarka
> 2009: 411).

One might add that this process is usefully explained by
Gramsci's notion of hegemony, where the hegemonic entity
takes notice of and partially includes the interests and preoccupations of the groups over whom dominance is sought
in order to achieve a certain superficial consensus. This is a
way of avoiding ongoing and overt conflict with dominated
groups (conflicts which might lead to lasting weakening of
the dominant power), but concessions are only possible up
to a certain point. (e.g. Gramsci 1971: 161)

De Gaulle also adopted themes which were more associated with opposition groups, in particular when he periodi-
cally raised the possibility of introducing what he described
as *participation*, and most notably in the midst of the uprising in May 1968. This idea, which never translated into
practice, was presented in the form of an industrial relations
strategy which allowed workers a share in profits, capital or
management of the firm for which they worked, or all three.
Participation superficially emulated more social-democratic
arrangements associated with Scandinavia in particular,
but for de Gaulle it came in the form of association of capital
and labour based on patronage and was envisaged at the
level of the individual firm rather than nationally. This was
a prime example of a populist borrowing of a notion from
the left and reinterpreting it in such a way that it served (or
would have done) the interests of the right.

The third general tactic employed by Sarkozy was to
push through reforms rapidly and simultaneously, again in
order to confuse, disorient and divide opponents. As I mentioned in the introduction to this chapter, one of the most
striking characteristics of the first eighteen months of the
Sarkozy presidency was a quite deliberately bewildering
number of different reforms. Some of them were in the end
fully implemented, but a number were withdrawn and
many were implemented in a highly altered form. In a pro-

cess described by the not unsympathetic Elie Cohen (2010) as 'carpet bombing' which he argues is intended to achieve a state of disorientation, demoralisation and bewilderment among adversaries, the president put forward an unprecedented number of reforms during his first eighteen months in office, many of them inspired at root by a desire to follow the Anglo-American neo-liberal economic model. In brief (pending closer examination of some new legislation, below), these included: reform of the 35-hour week, the introduction of Sunday shopping, substantial changes to established pension schemes for train and underground train drivers, devolution of budgets in higher education and changes to the school curriculum accompanied by job cuts in schools. Other proposals were often informed by the high profile law and order agenda, including tighter laws on immigration and expulsion of a greater number of illegal immigrants (*sans papiers*). Sarkozy also sought easier recourse to imprisonment, the stepping up of surveillance procedures, and a general overhaul of the legal system.

The fourth general tactic was to compromise through government-led — and often Sarkozy-led — negotiation with interested parties and to make concessions to them. These were concessions to groups and individuals whose conditions were likely to deteriorate as a result of new legislation, as we shall see in the discussion of the reform programme below. A close advisor on industrial relations and other work-related matters, Raymond Soubie, commented that 'it is better to have a reform of which 80 per cent gets through than have 100 per cent of a reform that gets rejected by the two sides of industry' (in Cahuc and Zylberberg 2009: 20). Finance Minister Christine Lagarde also argued that an approach involving compromise has meant that there has been 'not one hundred per cent on each and every count, but generally about eighty per cent because we had to accommodate resistance to change' (in Hall and Hollinger 2009: 13).

Sarkozy's approach was thus not that of Margaret Thatcher in Britain in the 1980s; although many of their longer-term goals were similar, Sarkozy did not go to the brink with the key groups who opposed his reforms as did Thatcher with the miners in the mid-1980s. Instead, he sought a certain amount of compromise and conciliation, given that confrontation had gone so wrong in the past. To repeat, this apparently bizarre approach to ruling the country using a series of unconventional tactics is largely explained by a fear of being defeated on the streets. The combined effect of these four tactics was also to both reinforce Sarkozy's authority — as it seemed he was the only unifying factor in the programme of reform and the only one in overall control — and to disarm the opposition parties and opposition in society more generally. It also ensured that the news media talked almost exclusively of the president and of his reform programme. It is worth pointing out that none of these tactics were necessary from the point of view of achieving a majority in parliament in support of new legislation, where the UMP had a large majority. Rather, the tactics described above were a way of attempting to avoid grass roots protests, divide the opposition, and allow Sarkozy to consolidate his already substantial authority. However, this approach to the reform agenda also confused many who had voted for him and lost him a great deal of general support, according to opinion polls, especially among older people.

I will now examine in more detail the nature of and effect of Sarkozy's reform programme. Some of the goals of the UMP under Sarkozy were indeed achieved and this has meant that France is somewhat more akin to Britain and the USA, for example, than previously. However, I will argue in what follows that there were various problems which he encountered. The strategy of avoiding head-on confrontation with protesters meant that the reforms were made less effective than they might have been. Moreover, the banking crisis and subsequent more general economic crisis obliged a quasi-U-turn on the withdrawal of the state from the economy and, as in many other industrialised countries, France was obliged to pursue a more Keynesian route than had been expected or than was desired by the government.

In pursuit of the free economy:
work, business and labour relations

In the half-page preface to Sarkozy's presidential electoral programme, which is written in his own handwriting, he makes just one substantive point: 'France is experiencing a moral crisis: a crisis of work. The rehabilitation of work is at the heart of my presidential project' (Sarkozy 2007b: 1). Work (or labour, as both are translations of his word *travail*) and related words such as worker (*travailleur*) are of course strongly associated with the left. But they are also associated with a right-wing populist approach to the question of transformation; Philippe Pétain, for example, replaced the republican tryptich 'liberty, equality, fraternity' with 'work, family, homeland' (*travail, famille, patrie*) during the period of collaboration with the occupying Nazis. We have seen that de Gaulle invoked the idea of (quasi-worker) *participation* when he wanted to enhance his popular appeal. There was no possibility of mistaking Sarkozy — self-avowed leader during the election campaign of the 'unapologetic right' (*droite décomplexée*) — for a man of the left, but a preoccupation with the notion of work put him in a stronger position to appropriate some of the themes associated with it and thus to partially neutralise the left's and the trades unions' potential protest actions. If Sarkozy's approach to work were to be summed up in one sentence, it would be to reward hard work and to end a situation where the state, as he saw it, was protecting and cushioning some people far too much — and especially those who were in fact not working or not working hard — and the state was also contributing to preventing the freeing of markets which would help get France onto the path of greater competitivity again, which would itself create jobs. The message was thus highly divisive of ordinary working people and deeply populist in the way in which it was both conventionally right-wing and also designed to appeal to certain sections of the working class who were disillusioned with the left.

One of the most important changes regarding work was the law on Work, Employment and Purchasing Power (*Loi en faveur du travail, l'emploi et le pouvoir d'achat*, or TEPA), which was rushed through in the summer of 2007 and was designed as a flagship reform. It was described on the government website as a 'beacon' as far as new legislation was concerned, and 'designed to restore entirely the notion of work as a valued entity and a way of raising standards of living' (www.tepa.minefe.gouv.fr). One important element of the law was the exemption from taxation and social charges for overtime — that is for hours worked above the statutory thirty-five per week — which had the effect of putting the onus on employees to work harder in order to increase their income, rather than on employers to pay more, which was very much in the logic of Sarkozy's election slogan 'work more to earn more'. Not only was this designed to undermine the 35-hour week without increasing the legal maximum working time (which would have been opposed vigorously by trade unions and others) it also discouraged employers from taking on more workers, given that extending working time for those currently employed was a far cheaper option.

Other aspects of this law which were designed to appeal to the business community and the rich in particular included the substantial lowering of inheritance tax. Perhaps most importantly there was also a new cap on taxation (a *bouclier fiscal*, or 'fiscal shield'), which introduced an upper limit on taxation of 50 per cent of income which in effect abolishes wealth tax. Measures contained in the same law which were aimed at wooing the less well-off included the removal of taxation on mortgage interest payments, allowing university students to work tax-free, and putting constraints on the most extravagant golden handshakes for company bosses. It was indeed intended as a flagship change and was described by its supporters as a series of measures that would improve the lives of many individuals in many different social groups and also stimulate economic growth and prosperity, measures which would compensate for the substantial reduction in income to the public purse. It was, however, widely seen as a law which greatly favoured the rich and privileged, with a few minor concessions to the less wealthy.

There was a host of smaller changes which were designed to help businesses. For example, the local business investment tax, the *taxe professionelle*, was abolished, which has left some local authorities short of funds. Another example is a certain relaxation of laws regarding shop opening hours on Sundays, with the most liberal regulations applying in tourist areas and the main shopping centres of major cities.

In tandem with these measures to encourage free enterprise there came an attempt to both shrink and shake up the public sector. It was announced, for example, that only one in two retiring civil servants would be replaced, and the civil service in France includes teachers, police and social workers, for example. In early 2010, Minister of the Budget, Public Accounts and the Civil Service, Eric Woerth commented: 'We have reduced the number of civil servants by 100,000 over the past three years. We could not have done otherwise' (In *Le Nouvel observateur* 28 January–2 February: 14). A further 100,000 public sector jobs were due to be shed between 2010 and 2013 (*Le Monde* 1.07.10). As part of this shake-up, the health service was substantially reorganised and the Post Office was prepared for partial privatisation and opening up for competition from other providers.

One of the most contentious areas of change was in education. In higher education, substantial changes were planned and many of them implemented, including budgetary devolution, financial control over buildings, greater power for university vice chancellors and encouragement of campus improvements via public-private partnerships. There were long and bitter strikes in universities in response to these proposals during the entire 2008–09 academic year, both on the part of university lecturers and by students, in what was almost certainly the most intense unrest in the higher education sector since 1968. Nevertheless, the most important elements of the reform went ahead, although the government decided against trying to force through the introduction of higher tuition fees in universities, a proposed change which had been defeated on several previous occasions. In primary and secondary schools there were also lengthy disputes in response both to substantial job cuts and proposals for a new approach to training school teachers.

After the first eighteen months of frenetic reforms, the recession altered the course of the Sarkozy programme. Having been an enthusiastic supporter of the free market (albeit with some reservations), the president resorted to a highly interventionist approach in response to the crisis, despite declaring in early 2008 that 'the coffers are empty' and he put together a reflation package for the French economy and he even announced, at the end of 2009 a 35 billion Euro loan to universities and museums in order to guarantee and enhance their future prospects. It was clear that France's large state sector and a more protectionist orientation than some other countries had helped shield the country from some of the worst effects. The *Financial Times* (10.11.09) put this as follows:

> The recession has been less severe in France than in any other large European economy, with a contraction of between 2 per cent and 2.25 per cent in 2009, according to government forecasts. The welfare state ... has proved its worth, softening the worst effects of the downturn and helping prop up consumption.

Liêm Hoang-Ngoc (2009: 433) argues that there was an undisputed return to Keynesian economic policy in response to the banking crisis and ensuing recession, and that this constituted a *rupture* with the much-trumpeted *rupture* of the early period of the Sarkozy presidency. Having been the apostle of the free market, privatisation and the deregulation of markets, the president then became 'an apologist for protectionism', albeit with some signs of continuity. Although this is perhaps a slightly exaggerated conclusion to draw, there is no doubt that there was a significant change of strategy and that the original plans had worn thin.

By June 2010 there were plans to raise the retirement age from sixty for both men and women to sixty-two by 2018 and increase the number of years' work required to receive a full pension from 40.5 to at least 41.5. These proposed measures prompted widespread protests, including national days of action on both 24 June and 7 September 2010, when millions took to the streets in towns and cities all over France. It seemed likely that taxes would be raised as well, in some form or another. Even before the economic crisis properly set in, the measures taken by government certainly did not produce the economic 'growth shock' which Sarkozy had wanted and which he had said he was going to trigger by reducing taxes, making labour law less tight, changing laws regarding trade union activity in the work place, and so on. The projected growth rate for 2008 was 2.25 per cent and the rate at which the economy finally grew was 0.9 per cent (Ngoc 2009: 427). Moreover, by the end of 2008 unemployment was rising and by summer 2010 was at a level which was over 10 per cent of the active population.

As far as industrial relations were concerned, the government quickly introduced legislation to guarantee a minimum level of public transportation during strikes, a mandatory two days' notice before strikes take place and a requirement that strikers should be consulted by secret ballot one week into a strike in order to test whether there is still majority support for the action. Sarkozy also insisted that the two sides of industry negotiate regarding a new work contract that would abolish the distinction between a permanent contract and a fixed-term contract, with less legal protection against dismissal for newer workers. This was in some ways reminiscent of the ill-fated CPE proposals under Chirac (discussed in Chapter Three). Agreement on this was reached (with the exception of the CGT trade union confederation) in January 2008; in a final text which fulfilled most of the employers' wishes, there was to be a new type of contract governing fixed-term employment, an initial period of employment during which dismissal was relatively straightforward, and measures allowing the ending of employment after agreement between employer and employee. In all, this was a series of measures which was greatly favoured by MEDEF and other employers' organisations. Finally, since August 2008 there is a new law regarding representation of trade unions, which lays down that unions must have 10 per cent membership in a firm and

8 per cent overall in order to be able to sign agreements. This gives more power to the large CGT and *Confédération française démocratique du travail* (CFDT) organisations and less to smaller ones, namely *Confédération française des travaillers chrétiens* (CFTC), *Confédération française de l'encadrement -Confédération générale des cadres* (CFE-CGC), *Confédération générale du travail-Force ouvrière* (CGT-FO), *Union nationale des syndicats autonomes* (UNSA) and *Solidares, unitaires et démocratiques* (SUD), so that in theory, this law encourages recomposition.

In another area which had tremendous symbolic significance, the new government managed to reform quickly certain public sector pension schemes, mainly in transport and energy (for workers in national railways, underground trains, gas and electricity). These schemes were known as 'special regimes' (*régimes spéciaux*) and were seen by some as unduly generous as in some cases they allowed workers to retire in their fifties. Workers in these sectors are among the most militant in France and for Sarkozy and his colleagues this was a crucial area. The new law meant that the period over which contributions were made was harmonised with the private sector, but in order to reach an agreement the government compromised and included bonus payments in pension calculations, which was a costly concession designed to avoid further industrial action and in order to persuade the more militant CGT trade union confederation to sign an agreement. Indeed, Sarkozy himself went out of his way to meet union leaders regularly regarding these changes, insisting that some workers would receive compensation for reduction in pension payments or having to work longer.

There were certainly protests against many of these new measures, including a wave of public sector strikes as early as autumn 2007 in response to pension reform proposals and threats of job cuts. There were also days of action organised by the trade unions against various proposals, most notably in May 2008 (against extending the period over which employees made pension contributions), January and June 2009 (against job losses and in defence of living standards) and June and September 2010 (over proposed pension changes). In April 2008 school students demonstrated against proposed job losses in education in a wave of marches which had well over a million participants nationwide. But it would appear that the various tactics mentioned above on the part of the Sarkozy regime did indeed help achieve their objectives to the extent that none of the proposed new laws was defeated by protest action, by contrast with what happened under Jacques Chirac. The headline result was therefore good for the government.

In the longer term, however, it might become clear that changes under Sarkozy have not been as thorough as intended or has been claimed by the right. Pierre Cahuc and André Zylberberg (2009) make a detailed examination of the economic and social reform programme and argue that the Sarkozy approach is precisely about avoiding reform being defeated by protests, as it had been in the past; it was necessary to tread extremely carefully, as 'any resorting to force is doomed to failure' (*Ibid.*: 12). The strategy followed, then, was one of stifling opposition by having many new laws under consideration at the same time and therefore both promoting confusion and achieving fragmentation of the opposing forces. This was followed by a certain amount of conciliation in order to avoid too much conflict and possible defeat, without losing sight of the bigger picture. Cahuc and Zylberberg argue that, given the degree of concessions made on each new piece of legislation, it is very difficult to determine to what extent the original goals were achieved. They examine the new measures concerning the special pension schemes in the public transport and energy sectors, for example, which they point out was the 'mother of all battles' for Sarkozy and that his credibility would have been destroyed — and he would have gone down the same road of perceived immobility as Chirac — had the reform entirely failed. It is very doubtful, they argue, that any money was saved as a result of the reform, but the essential point was to create the appearance of change, while the workers concerned lost very little and might even have gained a little, which is why the reforms were passed after only nine days of strikes (*Ibid.*: 19). If the other economic and social reforms are examined carefully, they argue, they almost all failed to achieve their goals because the groups concerned, who knew the issues so well, often outsmarted the government during the consultation process. These groups therefore emerged victors from the reforms. Moreover, the Thomas More think tank, based in Brussels, found in late 2009 that Sarkozy had not implemented anything like the full complement of reforms intended to be in place by that stage and that many of those there were in place were watered-down (www.institut-thomas-more.org).

The truth regarding the actual degree of change achieved by Sarkozy will probably not become clear for some time, and the economic crisis has blurred the picture considerably. But there is little doubt — particularly in light of the work done by Cahuc and Zylberberg — that the changes in the domain of economic and social policy are less far-reaching than either Sarkozy and his colleagues (or indeed many of his opponents) claim. Nevertheless, there is also little doubt that the conditions for doing business in France are now more similar to those of Britain and the USA in particular, but that the dream of a self-regulating economy, dynamised by a spirit of free enterprise and liberated from official constraints has been thwarted in various ways, not least by capitalist crisis caused by precisely these sorts of free-marketeer conditions.

Sarkozy's radically pro-American foreign policy is significant as part of an effort to enhance France's image as a business-friendly, free enterprise-oriented country which is moving away from perceived cultural and business isolationism and towards being a full participant in the global market. From the word go he was keen to make this clear and the appointment of the pro-American Bernard Kouchner as Foreign Minister sent a clear message in that regard. Sarkozy spent two weeks on holiday in the US in summer 2007, during which time he met President Bush and his family at Bush's summer home in Kennebunkport and since then he has made several state visits to the US. On the first state visit, in November 2007, he addressed the

Congress and received a standing ovation, in recognition of the apparent watershed in respect of US-French relations which Sarkozy becoming president represented. Final confirmation of this new direction in foreign relations came when France re-joined the NATO integrated command structure after forty-three years of working outside of it; France withdrew from the structure in 1966 when de Gaulle was president.

The autocrat and the strong state

Sarkozy's presidency has seen him both exert a tight personal grip on the nation, and alongside this style and practice of authoritarian leadership there has been an increasingly strong and authoritarian state, with particular emphasis on law and order. We have seen that his autocratic approach meant involving himself personally in as many areas as he possibly could, in a constant flurry of all-seeing, all-knowing, relentless activism. Power was concentrated in the Elysée Palace with a team of advisers permitted to talk to media while the government itself was marginalised and seemed devalued.

This style of government meant that the president did indeed appear as supreme ruler, with both Prime Minister François Fillon and parliament becoming almost incidental to the governing process. Jean-Pierre Dubois, President of the French League for Human Rights, suggests that in the first year of Sarkozy's presidency, democracy was 'asphyxiated by a President-Sun-King (*président-soleil*) who runs the state like a personal undertaking in a jet-set atmosphere which is free of any complex or scruple' (Dubois, 2008a: 6). This perception of Sarkozy as a leader seeking to appear as incarnating the will of the people is at times expressed in more positive terms by close colleagues, and perhaps most clearly by Rachida Dati, at the time Minister for Justice, when she explained that 'supreme legitimacy is held by the French people who elected Nicolas Sarkozy in order to restore authority … and magistrates carry out justice in the name of this supreme legitimacy' (in *Ibid.*: 6). At times this manic, controlling omni-presence seemed to bring on delusions of omnipotence, with comments such as '[w]hether growth is at 1.9 or 2.3 per cent doesn't change much in the end. What I want is three per cent.' (in Hauser, 2008: 29). The aggression which appeared to be part of this approach to the presidency was often apparent, but perhaps most notably when in February 2008, in response to a man in a crowd at an agricultural fair who refused to shake his hand, he responded by saying: 'sod off then, loser!' (in *Le Monde*, 26.02.08). This was shown on television and was then watched by tens of thousands of viewers on YouTube.

There were various court cases where Sarkozy pursued opponents legally, including in the Clearstream Affair regarding alleged tax evasion and money laundering, where the arch-rival of Sarkozy and former Prime Minister Dominique de Villepin was on trial for complicity in false denunciation but acquitted in late October 2009. As de Villepin arrived at the courthouse for the first hearing on 21 September that year, he declared to the press: 'I am here because of the determination of one man, Nicolas Sarkozy, who is also president of the French republic'. In the course of the hearings, he commented: '[T]he finger of Nicolas Sarkozy has been pointed at me and at the President of the Republic. There is a desire, a determination to destroy a political opponent.' (*Le Monde* 25–26.10.10) This case was certainly seen by many as an example of the extremes to which the president would go in his determination to be undisputed leader of the right. The obverse of this is the apparent nepotism on the part of Sarkozy; the most extreme example of this came when there seemed to be high-level influence when his 23-year old son Jean Sarkozy came within a hair's breadth of becoming head of the state-run organisation that oversees *La Défense*, the business area on the western edge of Paris (*Financial Times* 10.11.09). This district was to have even greater importance in the context of *Grand Paris*, a Sarkozy-led plan which envisaged an enhanced influence of Paris in a largely business-motivated scheme to improve transportation links and buildings infrastructure in the Paris region and all the way to the coast at Le Havre, and which was to be controlled in highly centralised way.

A particularly important manner in which Sarkozy asserted his influence was via increased control over the media, using both formal and informal means. Certainly, other presidents of the Fifth Republic had sought to influence the media directly and Mitterrand had, for example, replaced people in important positions in the broadcast media with allies and friends. De Gaulle was in almost direct control of the state-run *Office de la radiodiffusion-télévision française* (ORTF) broadcasting corporation for many years and the ORTF presented news of both France and the world only in a way in which the General approved (Vassallo 2005). Sarkozy, via various means, was attempting to approach this degree of influence on broadcast media in particular, but also to some extent on the press.

In a book entitled *Petits Arrangements entre amis. Le Parrain des médias* ('Little deals between friends. The godfather of the media'), Noël Mamère and Patrick Farbiaz (2009) argue that the fact that Sarkozy grew up in and was for many years mayor of the wealthy Paris suburb Neuilly was of great importance for his careful cultivation of powerful figures in the French media. A number of the media tycoons in Sarkozy's circle of close friends indeed either lived or had their company's head office in Neuilly. Moreover, five of the numerous rich and famous guests at the meal at Fouquet's restaurant organised in order to celebrate Sarkozy's presidential victory were key figures in the media world, with other substantial business interests as well. These five powerful individuals were: Bernard Arnault, who owns the financial newspaper *Les Echos* and the world number one luxury goods company LVMH (a witness at Sarkozy and his second wife Cécilia's wedding); Vincent Bolloré, proprietor of the television channel *Direct 8* and free newspaper *Direct soir* as well as chairman of the huge international publicity and communications company Havas; Martin Bouygues, owner of the commercial television network, TF1 (also a witness at Sarkozy and Cécilia's wedding and godfather to their son Louis); Serge Dassault, owner of the right-leaning newspaper *Le Figaro* and head of both aeronautics group Dassault; and Nicolas Beytout, former editor of both *Les Echos* and *Le Figaro* and head of the *Groupe des echos*, the media wing of LVMH. Other powerful media figures among Sarkozy's acolytes include: Arnaud Lagardère, whose Lagardère group owns the news and celebrity magazine *Paris match*, the Sunday newspaper *Le Journal de Dimanche*, and the commercial radio station *Europe 1*; Jean-Claude Dassier, head of news at TF1 until July 2009 and former head of 24-hour news channel LCI and whose son Arnaud ran Sarkozy's presidential internet campaign; and Jean-Pierre Elkabbach, former chair of *Europe 1* and head of Lagardère News. (Kuhn 2010; Mamère and Farbiaz 2009.)

In addition to what might be described as this informal media-business-friendship complex, Raymond Kuhn (*Ibid.*: 3-5) suggests that there are three other ways in which Sarkozy has sought to manage and influence the media. First, the president works closely with professional communication advisors. For example, Franck Louvrier, one of the architects of the 2007 presidential campaign and a close collaborator on the media and other areas of communication since 1997, has a daily meeting with the president and other members of the inner circle of advisors. Other close aides in this domain include Catherine Pégard, a former journalist for the magazine *Le Point*, Alain Minc, previously chair of the board at *Le Monde* and Pierre Giacometti, one time head of one of France's best-known opinion polling organisations, Ipsos. Second, and perhaps most concretely, Sarkozy has sought to assert formal presidential control over public broadcasting. In 2009 there were far-reaching reforms in this domain which affected both funding and organisation, via which the president of the republic regained the right to nominate the chief executive of the state-owned *France télévisions* and *Radio France*. As Kuhn (*Ibid.*: 5) points out, '[t]his mode of appointment returns public broadcasting to the era prior to President François Mitterrand's 1982 reform that first established a regulatory authority for broadcasting, one of whose powers was to appoint the heads of the public service companies'. Third, Sarkozy has always gone to great lengths to develop direct relations with political journalists. Very much part of the hyperactive and controlling conduct for which he is well-known, individual attention with regard to journalists can be both positive and negative, ranging from cultivating ongoing friendships to outright intimidation, according to Magoudi (2009).

This intense preoccupation with the media is, of course, to some extent common to all advanced capitalist societies. With decreasing interest in politics on the part of ordinary people goes trivialisation of the question of politics as expressed in the media. Preoccupation with politicians' personal lives becomes ever more dominant and this in turn tends to reduce politics to a series of game-like contests between leaders, rather than a process for deciding how power is distributed in a more profound way (e.g. King 2002). In almost all advanced capitalist societies, then, the image of political leaders in the media is crucial, and teams specializing in marketing and public relations ever more important to the success or failure of a leader; the logic of this is to establish a direct bond between leader and electorate with a reduced need for the traditional intermediary of the political party, and a tendency to marginalize other intermediary elements, including parliament.

A revealing and highly significant area of change during Sarkozy's presidency has indeed been in the domain of the constitution of the Fifth Republic. These reforms were presented as ones which would correct the dominance of the president and his government at the expense of parliament and indeed the ordinary citizen, dominance which had been enshrined in law since 1958. In fact, little has been done to weaken the president's powers or strengthen parliament and, on balance, the contrary is true. Certainly (following Szarka 2009), a revised Article 48 of the constitution stipulates that a quarter of parliamentary sittings must be devoted to consideration of public policies. It is also argued that there is reduced executive power because revisions to

Article 49-3, which allowed the government to make a bill a 'question of confidence' in the National Assembly, meaning that to defeat the bill there must be a motion of censure against the government, tabled within 24 hours and supported by an absolute majority of members. But revisions to Article 49, combined with powers of 'accelerated procedure' (Article 45) mean continued tight governmental control over parliamentary procedure. As far as presidential powers are concerned, changes to the highly controversial Article 16 mean that recourse to special powers in times of 'national emergency' is less-readily available. Also, after the Sarkozy reforms an individual may hold presidential office twice at the most. But the most important constitutional change allows the president to address both lower and upper house together, once per year, at the Palace of Versailles. This—almost regal—new practice is followed immediately by a debate, but without the president being present and the speech is not subject to a motion of confidence. The speech, highly reminiscent of the annual State of the Union speech by the President of the USA, doubtless undermines the authority of the prime minister. Szarka (*Ibid.*: 415) sums up his views on the changes as follows:

> Thus the president is not accountable to parliament. Presidential unaccountability, which had been custom and practice in the Fifth Republic, is now engraved in the Constitution. [Moreover, the] new citizen rights are extremely limited. The proposal to institute a people's right to initiate a referendum was watered down: a referendum can be called if supported by a fifth of parliamentarians and subscribed by a tenth of the electorate (art. 11). The copious changes to the minutiae of the constitution coupled with unwillingness to touch its core tenets serve to confirm its main thrust—which is the supremacy of the presidency.

The strongly Bonapartist characteristics of the constitution of the Fifth Republic, which involve concentration of power in the executive wing of the state, thus not only remain intact but are, if anything, reinforced.

Sarkozy has become increasingly associated with a more repressive state and a more severe law and order agenda as the months and the years of his presidency have gone by. As far as the justice system is concerned, the approach has certainly been to send a harsher message than had been the case before, with recommendations for longer minimum sentences for re-offenders, proposals to put certain convicts in detention centres at the end of their terms in prison (a proposal which was partially thrown out by the Constitutional Council) and generally an approach to sentencing which has meant that the prison population has continued to grow. The government found itself in open conflict with much of the judiciary early on in its term when it announced it would abolish France's independent investigating magistrates and transfer the responsibility for investigations to the state prosecutor's office, which would not be independent from the Ministry of Justice, thus suggesting that the government might become involved in certain legal cases. Also as part of a clear law and order agenda, in summer 2010 the president promised changes that would enable the withdrawal of family allowance payments and even imprisonment of parents whose children persistently stay away from school.

The Sarkozy presidency has also been closely associated with a harsher approach to the question of immigration. The creation of a ministry entitled Ministry of Immigration, Integration, National Identity and Development Solidarity was part of this, and designed in particular to consolidate support from former FN voters. There has been a drive to increase the numbers of expulsions of illegal immigrants (*sans papiers*) from France. When moving from the Ministry of Immigration to the Ministry of Labour in January 2009, Brice Hortefeux (one of Sarkozy's most loyal supporters) announced that 29,796 illegal immigrants had been forcibly repatriated in 2008, amounting to almost 4000 more than the original target for the year. This was, he commented, 'an unprecedented result, an increase of 28.5 per cent' over the previous twelve months (in Fouteau 2010: 160). When Besson took over the ministry in January 2009, he announced a target of 26,000 compulsory repatriations per year and in summer 2010 government ministries organised the breaking up of many Roma camps and very quickly deported thousands of Roma. This was condemned by both the United Nations and by the European Commission, which pointed out that discrimination on grounds of ethnic origin is illegal in European Union member states. The same year, the government launched highly controversial debates both about the nature of French national identity and the legitimacy or otherwise of wearing the face-covering Islamic veil in public.

Various incidents and miscalculations have served to discredit the government, its ministers and the president himself in the domain of relations associated with questions of ethnicity. In 2010 Hortefeux was found guilty of racial insult and ordered to pay a fine of 750 Euros and donate 2000 Euros to an anti-racist group for making a remark at a UMP summer school in 2009 when posing with a dark-skinned young man; he said: 'There always has to be one. When there is one that's OK. It's when there are a lot that there are problems.' He appealed against the verdict.

The Sarkozy regime's approach towards relations with developing countries and the history of colonialism appeared close to that of the extreme right when Sarkozy made a speech in Dakar on 26 July 2007 during his first presidential visit to Africa and when he insisted that 'Africa has its own share of responsibility in its own misfortunes'. He went on to say that:

> The problem with Africa is that the African has not become part of history. The African, who for millennia has lived according to the seasons and whose ideal is to live in harmony with nature, knows only the eternal cycle of time structured by a repetitive and endless rhythm of the same movements and the same words ... [moreover] colonialism is not responsible for all Africa's problems today ... bloody wars which Africans wage amongst themselves ... genocides...dictators...fanaticism, corruption ... [colonialism] is not responsible for the waste and the pollution ... In this approach to life, where everything constantly begins again, there is no place for human adventure or for the idea of progress ... The challenge for Africa is to enter more into history. (Sarkozy 2007f)

In response to this speech there was outrage not only among many African leaders but also among French people of many different political persuasions, a reaction which prompted the publication of several collections of essays (e.g. Rey 2008).

Municipal, European and regional elections

The extreme personalisation of power which the Sarkozy presidency represents means that not only have the obviously *ad hominem* problems with the president reflected badly on him, but they have affected the right as a whole. By spring 2008, Sarkozy was already unpopular with many French people, for reasons which we have explored at some length. In the municipal elections in March that year, the left—in particular the PS—won a clear victory, achieving control of a substantial majority of towns, cities and administrative *départements*, and gaining numerous large cities, including Caen, Metz, Reims, Saint-Etienne, Strasbourg and Toulouse. Although the right did not suffer the colossal defeat it had feared, the fact that only 35 per cent of the electorate turned out to vote (the highest rate of abstention in a local election since 1959) was seen as an indictment of the measures taken by government since May 2007, but also of the political class more generally. Nevertheless, Sarkozy and his Prime Minister François Fillon insisted that the reform programme should continue unaffected.

In the European elections of June 2009, the UMP did far better than expected and won thirty seats out of a total seventy-two, with the ecologists and the centre-left (mainly PS) parties winning fourteen each. By contrast with the 2008 local elections, then, this was seen as a consolidation of the right's position, which Sarkozy announced would allow them to move forward quickly on changes to pension arrangements and the environment. What these results seemed to demonstrate was that while the government and the centre-right more generally were not being punished and did, if anything, have the support of a substantial proportion of voters, this contrasted starkly with many French people's perception of Sarkozy, whose popularity rate remained low. This was consistent with the results of opinion polls which suggested that whilst the president was very unpopular, Prime Minister François Fillon was far more popular (perhaps in part because he was so side-lined by the president).

The regional elections of March 2010, which were seen as an important mid-term test of the presidency's popularity, were an unmitigated disaster not only for Sarkozy himself, but also for the UMP and the centre-right more generally. In the second round of the elections, the left received 55.1 per cent of the vote, the right 35.4 per cent and the FN 9.4 per cent. The left (mainly PS) won 21 out of 22 regions in metropolitan France, the only victory for the right being in Alsace. Certainly, many governments in many countries do badly in mid-term elections, but this was an exceptionally poor performance for the right and in particular for the UMP. The gap between left and right voters had not been as large since the landslide victory for the Socialists in the parliamentary elections of 1981, after Mitterrand became president of the republic. The second part of this major blow for Sarkozy and the UMP was that the FN appeared to be gaining ground again, at the expense of the UMP. In the second round of these elections, the FN was present in twelve regions and received an average 17 per cent of the vote in these. The president of the FN, Jean-Marie Le Pen, received the highest score for the party, with 22.9 per cent of the vote in the southern Provence-Alpes-Côte d'Azur while his daughter and heir apparent Marine Le Pen received 22.2 per cent in the northern Nord-Pas-de-Calais region. This was a particularly heavy blow, as Sarkozy had won in part because he had managed to attract the vote of the FN and it was clear that disaffected blue-collar voters were once again gravitating towards the extreme right; over one in five blue-collar workers voted FN in the first round. The general disaffection with politics was reflected in a particularly high rate of abstention. The rate of abstention was at 48.9 per cent in the first round and 53.6 in the second, compared with an average (i.e. both rounds combined) 34.3 per cent in the regional elections in 2004; younger and blue-collar voters abstained in particularly large numbers, with 72 per cent of

18 to 34 year-olds staying away from the polls, and 69 per cent of blue-collar workers (*Le Monde* 23.03.10: 4)

Immediately after the regional elections, the distinctly right-leaning and normally UMP-sympathetic news magazine *Le Point* (25.03.10) ran the following front-page headline, over a photograph of a despondent-looking president: 'The Sarkozy Tragedy'. It launched a blistering attack on the Sarkozy method of government and in its editorial it accused the president of extreme autocracy and of neglecting the views of both ordinary *députés* (MPs) and ministers, which meant that in personifying power he personified failure. This, the editorial continued, was a failure which came in part from manic, simultaneous legislation which left many former supporters lost and bewildered, not to mention outraged at his attempt to parachute his own son into a position of considerable power at *La Défense*. Elsewhere the magazine listed numerous ways in which Sarkozy had publically offended many groups in French society, including magistrates ('peas in a pod'), bankers (who were greedy), researchers (who discovered nothing), the military (which was irresponsible), strikers (whose strikes no-one noticed any more), Chirac (a useless *roi-fainéant*), Bretons (whom he 'didn't give a damn about'), farmers (collectively insulted by the 'sod off, loser!' remark), diplomats ('pretentious') and intellectuals who knew only how to lounge about in Parisian cafes (*Ibid.*: 44).

The lessons Sarkozy drew from these election results were rather different, it seemed, from those the *Le Point* articles might have suggested. In the remainder of the spring and summer there was greater emphasis on questions of law and order, 'delinquency', the question of immigration controls and the expulsion of illegal — as well as some legal, Roma — immigrants, questions which often seemed to be connected in the eyes of the government and Sarkozy, in a way that was no doubt calculated to appeal to voters with sympathies with the extreme right.

The results of the regional elections of course gave hope to the *Parti socialiste* in particular and it seemed at last that the PS and the rest of the left had some chance of winning the elections of 2012, assuming it could find the right candidate and unite behind her or him. I return to the question of the left in the next chapter.

Conclusions

An examination of the policy agenda, the behaviour and the fortunes of the Sarkozy regime allows us to draw some preliminary conclusions regarding the nature and meaning of this period in French political history. Sarkozy as president has continued to be highly activist, autocratic and controlling, an approach which is of course enabled by the constitution of the Fifth Republic, which affords a supremely important role to the head of state. He has fully exploited the previously existing provisions of the constitution both in his general style of leadership and in the day-to-day practice of governing the country; many analysts sum up this approach by suggesting that Sarkozy has been in effect simultaneously both president and prime minister. But Sarkozy has indeed extended his formal powers by introducing changes to the constitution which allow the president greater influence, in particular via the annual address to a joint meeting of the upper and lower houses of parliament at the Palace of Versailles. Another general approach has been to attempt to blur the boundaries between left and right, in part by poaching individuals from the centre-left to act either as ministers or policy advisors and in part by placing emphasis on general themes which are associated with the left. The most obvious example of this is a preoccupation with the question of work, which was a leitmotif of the Sarkozy presidential campaign and has also been at the heart of the governmental programme.

These characteristics — autocracy, attempting to blur the boundaries between left and right and a preoccupation with the question of work — help explain why Sarkozy won and continues to enjoy consistent support from the right and from the business community. Certainly, other presidents since 1958 have behaved in similar manner in some respects. But the major innovation as far as the Sarkozy presidency is concerned is to place centre-stage the promotion of business — in particular big business — and profit, and to place such an emphasis on the importance of making money. Sarkozy's background in the wealthy Parisian suburb of Neuilly, his close friendships with big business people and media moguls, and his close association with the employers' organisation MEDEF all pointed to an ongoing and systematic defence of business interests at the expense of the interests both of ordinary working people and the public sector. As if to underline this point, Sarkozy's own salary as president increased from 101,000 to 240,000 Euros per year soon after he took office. The crucial law on Work, Employment and Purchasing Power (TEPA), passed within a few months of Sarkozy coming to power, was designed to reward the rich and to encourage workers well down the social hierarchy to work harder. The public sector, meanwhile, was to be reduced substantially, although the role of the state was not by any means eroded to the extent it was under Margaret Thatcher in Britain, for example.

As we saw in Chapter Three, some reforms along these lines had been attempted by previous governments, but they had often been defeated on the street. Sarkozy, however, appeared to combine the hunger for personalised power with a neo-liberal agenda which persuaded big business and the almost-united right not only to back him as a presidential candidate but to offer continued support in the often complex tactical manoeuvres involving negotiations (and some concessions) on may fronts and in ways which sometimes seemed to contradict each other.

The economic crisis of course came as a major setback for the Sarkozy agenda. The pursuit of a largely self-regulating economy became ever-less popular and indeed unworkable as the extent of the crisis became clearer, and as the threat of higher unemployment became more real. It soon became evident that France's relatively large public sector and the strong role for the state in the economy was helping the country to weather the recession better than many other advanced capitalist countries. Embracing a more traditionally French, even quasi-Keynesian economic policy was thus a necessary but very bitter pill for Sarkozy and the rest of the right to swallow.

It was not from strikes and demonstrations that Sarkozy had the most to fear, although there had been bitter disputes in various companies in the first year of his presidency, some involving kidnapping of managing directors of firms where there were widespread redundancies, combined with numerous national days of action organised by the trade union movement against the reform programme. Sarkozy, his advisors and his government seemed to have reduced the impact of the labour movement by playing a cunning tactical game, reforming fast and furiously but making concessions in order to win the overall result. Certainly, the huge protests against pension reform in autumn 2010 were a real cause for alarm. But it was the profound and ongoing unpopularity of the president himself that was most damaging to the regime. It seemed that the tactics that had enabled a reduction of the impact of the trade unions and other interested parties came as part of a package which included Sarkozy's frequent public outbursts which were characterised by irascibility and were often insulting. A highly personalised approach to political change brought with it a personality whose many unappealing traits, including narcissism and a penchant for nepotism, meant that political change became increasingly tainted. This is indeed one of the many hazards associated with personalised, autocratic rule.

Chapter Five

Understanding the Sarkozy Phenomenon

In this book I have attempted to explain the rise of Nicolas
Sarkozy to the position of president of the republic and then
the behaviour and fortunes of Sarkozy and his allies once he
was president. I have suggested that the most useful analyt-
ical model to adopt when interpreting the Sarkozy phenomenon is that of Bonapartism, where as a result of a social,
economic and/or political crisis an individual is invested
with considerable power for a limited period of time in
order to achieve a particular set of objectives. Put succinctly,
the French business community and its associates had
become desperate for change and the bold and outspoken
figure of Sarkozy appeared capable of achieving enough
support in the wider French population to drive through
the reforms required in particular by the financial and
industrial elite. Certainly, he was in some respects a maverick and therefore a potential liability, even in the eyes of his
loyal followers, but other options (broadly associated with
the more softly-softly approach of Jacques Chirac)
appeared to have run out and it seemed necessary to resort
to more drastic measures. I have suggested that some of the
planned changes have indeed been brought about (albeit, as
it has turned out, often in partial fashion) and this has happened at great cost in other respects. But the longer-term
results may — even in the centre-right's own terms — be very
wide of the the initial objectives. In this concluding chapter I
draw the threads of the argument together, consider some

objections which might be raised to my line of argument
and look at other interpretations. To begin, I will make some
general remarks about the international and national
politico-economic context in which Sarkozy's rise to power
took place.

The societies and economies of advanced capitalist countries have passed through various stages since the Second
World War. The first stage was of intensive growth, based
in particular on consumer demand for products manufactured largely in highly-industrialised countries. This boom
period ended in economic crisis in the early-to-mid-1970s
and was followed by restructuring, which entailed moving
to more post-industrial, services- and information technol-
ogy-based economies with greater reliance on finance capital. By contrast with the post-war period, material
consumption depended increasingly on the importation of
goods manufactured cheaply in less developed countries. It
also relied on a reduction of the influence of the organised
labour movement in developed countries and the
archetypal example of this is Britain, where in the 1980s the
trade unions suffered lasting defeat at the hands of the
Thatcher government. Finally, the most recent stage of
politico-economic change — or at least presently-emerging
change — is one where on a global scale advanced capitalist
countries are facing another substantial challenge to the
economic and political status quo, in the form of the rise of
other states, especially Brazil, Russia, India and China.
Sometimes known as the BRIC nations, these countries look
likely to catch up rapidly with and eventually overtake the
US and its allies as measured in conventional economic
terms, perhaps as soon as the next few decades. An early
indication of the problems ahead for currently economi-
cally-dominant countries will almost certainly be a rise in
the price of imported goods due to increased labour costs in
developing countries. The global financial crisis has, of
course, added to these already-existing economic, and con-
sequently geo-political, problems.

The place of France in the recent and current trends in the
international political economy is, broadly speaking, along-

side other economically successful, largely post-industrial counties, who are grouped together in the OECD in order to defend their interests and even more exclusively in both the G20 and the G7 groups of highly developed countries. However, France still occupies a particular place amongst these countries because, although the proportion of employees in a trade union is small (probably less than 8 per cent of the working population in 2010), workers, their families and students in France are often more ready to take some sort of industrial action or other sorts of protest action than are many people in other countries which broadly share France's socio-economic characteristics. This is borne out by a survey which assesses the degree of harmony in workplace relations, where out of a total 139 countries, France is ranked near the very bottom of the table, at 129 (World Economic Forum 2010: 444). As we saw in Chapter Three, this militancy and volatility has meant that neo-liberal-oriented reform has been more difficult to achieve than it has been in many other countries and this has meant that, for example, there is a larger public sector in France and a higher degree of state protection than is often the case elsewhere. But just as the labour movement and those who ally themselves with the labour movement in France are more politicised, employers and their allies tend also to think and behave in a more politically-committed way. Recourse to the Bonapartist figure of Sarkozy, I have argued, is explained in large part by the desire on the part of the right wing and the business community in France to drive though modernising change and to attack what it sees as barriers to freedom of enterprise. This will make France — so the Sarkozy supporters' logic goes — more able to compete internationally and in the fullness of time more ready to deal with the increasing challenges of the rise of the BRIC economies.

But protest against the status quo in France also comes from the extreme right, notably regarding the question of immigration and immigrants' descendents, and support for the FN often comes from people who have lost out or are likely to lose out in the course of economic changes mentioned above. Sarkozy is also seen as a political leader who can absorb (or partially absorb) supporters of the FN into his own political movement and achieve a more unified approach on the right. We have seen that Sarkozy and his allies have often placed emphasis on what they claim is a moral crisis in France associated with the legacy of May 1968, and this new moralism is indeed associated with an attempt to lock the extreme right electorate into the centre-right camp. For the same reasons, there is strong emphasis on questions of immigration, law and order, and law-breaking on the part of young people, and the three areas are often presented as being intimately connected.

I discussed the nature of Bonapartism at some length in Chapter Two, both as a historical phenomenon and as a theory which helps enable an understanding of a particular situation. Characteristics of Bonapartism include: a leader promising salvation; a method of rule based on autocratic authoritarianism and voluntarism; the strengthening of the executive at the expense of the legislative; blurring boundaries between right and left; exploiting international issues for national benefit; attempts at a direct and populist relationship with the people; and a particular affinity with business and money. The history and theory of Bonapartism are, of course, closely related and history informs the theory to a large extent. However, with the exception of the original Bonapartist regimes (and for many analysts especially the regime of Napoleon III) there is no pure form of Bonapartism, but a variety of Bonapartisms which resemble each other enough in terms of underlying characteristics and which share enough common objectives and tactics to be usefully described as such. In other words, there is no ideal type of Bonapartism but a variety of types which are broadly similar. I have argued throughout that the Sarkozy campaign and the Sarkozy regime have sufficient elements of what is commonly understood as Bonapartism to merit this general classification and most importantly this approach enhances our understanding of the profounder nature of what is sometimes described as *Sarkozyism*.

One objection to the label Bonapartist might be that Sarkozy has not — at least since the immediate aftermath of his election as president — shared the degree of popularity among the French as a whole that, for example, Napoleon III enjoyed or even de Gaulle for that matter. Indeed, Sarkozy has been the least popular president of the republic since the beginning of the Fifth Republic in 1958, according to opinion polls (Teinturier 2010 and Appendix 5). However, his rise to the highest office took place on the crest of a wave of popularity which meant that in the first round of the presidential elections he received the highest ever number of votes in the Fifth Republic (nearly two million more than Ségolène Royal) and in the second round he received 53.1 per cent, which was almost as high as de Gaulle's record 54.5 per cent in 1965. Just as importantly, however, the centre-left was in substantial disarray and this appeared to strengthen Sarkozy's case for having a personal mandate to drive through significant structural change. Thus Sarkozy's actions partially reflect an initial popularity, despite this falling off rapidly soon after his election victory.

Another objection to the characterisation of Sarkozy as Bonapartist might be that in some important ways he is very much a conservative, career politician, with a background in party politics, ministerial office and leadership of the UMP party. He worked his way up through the ranks of the centre-right with a solid base in the wealthy Parisian suburban town, Neuilly-sur-Seine, where he was mayor for many years. Again, this traditional route is an important element in his rise to high office and this does set him apart from Napoleon III, Pétain or de Gaulle, for example, whose positions as outsiders coming in to offer salvation were in each case more striking. But this more conventional career route does not detract from the importance of the more extraordinary elements of Sarkozy's rise to power and rule and we have explored both strands — ordinary and extraordinary — in the overall make-up of Sarkozy's rise and rule. The mix of conventional, conservative politician, Bonapartist populist and in some respects far-right-leaning authoritarian has prompted some analysts to argue that

Sarkozy has managed to unite the three right-wing currents in France identified by René Rémond (1982), namely Bonapartist (mainly Gaullist), Orleanist (centre-right) and counter-revolutionary (extreme right), which had for many years been acting largely separately (e.g. Dupin 2007; Rozès 2007). I believe there is some truth in this, given what I have said above, but his particular orientation is nevertheless best explained by reference to the Bonapartist tradition than by either of the other currents.

In the above remarks I have given special attention to aspects of Sarkozy's rise to power and to his subsequent rule which are informed by or associated with France's exceptionally-radical modern history and the implication of this is indeed that France is in important ways different from many other advanced capitalist countries. However, in some other similar countries which also have liberal democratic systems of government there are also leaders with Sarkozy-like tendencies, although these tendencies are often less pronounced. Domenico Losurdo has argued that Bonapartism — at least in its milder forms which he describes as *soft* Bonapartism — is more prevalent than is usually thought (Losurdo 2007: 212–32). He argues that in many liberal democracies the formal political arrangements are in effect a 'political market' with largely passive 'elector-consumers', and where the idea of emancipation is now entirely absent from the prevailing concept of democracy. This, then, goes hand in hand with the emergence of soft Bonapartism, in part because leaders stand essentially on the same platform and there is a great deal of continuity from one administration to the next, even when there is a notional transition from centre-left to centre-right, or vice versa. In these politically-undifferentiated circumstances there is bound to be greater emphasis on the nature of the individual, especially where huge sums of money are needed in order to even stand in elections, let alone win them. Losurdo goes as far as arguing that soft Bonapartism is the triumphant regime in the twentieth century and that it is far more widespread than the more obvious examples, which include Thatcher, Blair and Clinton. Such an approach indeed allows us convincingly to go beyond the idea that a leader such as Sarkozy is somehow entirely at odds with the 'normal' politics of other contemporary liberal democracies (or with what preceded it in France, for that matter), and rather that he and his rule are on the same continuum with trends in the nature of political leadership more generally. I would argue, however, that Sarkozy (who was elected after the publication of Losurdo's book and is therefore not discussed in it) is at the more classic end of the Bonapartism spectrum, although no doubt not as near that classic end as de Gaulle, for example.

The next point I wish to make is that, as I have argued at greater length elsewhere (Hewlett 2003), stable and successful capitalism requires a certain depoliticisation of the people and that although this has been slower to arrive in France, it has certainly been more in evidence since the mid-1980s. This is a depoliticisation which, internationally, has been crucial to the neo-liberal era and which has characterised the capitalist system on a global level for several decades. In many liberal democracies indicators such as levels of abstention in elections and levels of party membership have been pointing very firmly in this direction, and France has on the whole been part of this trend. Despite the high level of participation in the presidential elections of 2007, the general participatory direction in France has been firmly downwards (Muxel 2007; Subileau 2001) and in the parliamentary elections of 2007 there was an all-time low turnout after the high rate of participation in the presidential elections. Thus the Sarkozy phenomenon, relying as it does on a certain portion of the electorate who will be attracted by simplistic, slogan-led responses (*rupture,* 'work more to earn more', and so on) to what are in fact highly complex problems, is drawing to an extent on a low level of political engagement.

With an increasingly passive and depoliticised electorate and dumbing down of the way in which the political agendas are presented goes the rise of the political leader as celebrity, not unlike the film or rock star. Sarkozy, again in an exaggerated way compared with many other political leaders, seemed particularly inclined in this direction in the period immediately after he was elected president, and to be emulating such stars with his *bling* fashion accessories, his lavish and ostentatious holidays, rich friends and his whirlwind romance followed by marriage to Carla Bruni. But the relative normality of the Sarkozy presidency alongside governments in other advanced capitalist societies is also highlighted by more sobre academic examination of what is sometimes termed 'presidentialism' or 'presidentialisation', a phenomenon that has been increasingly prevalent for some years. Poguntke and Webb, for example, suggest in their fourteen-country study that 'democratic political systems are coming to operate according to an essentially presidential logic, irrespective of their formal constitutional make-up' and that presidentialisation is evident in increased autonomy and power for leaders in both governmental structures and political parties, not to mention election campaigns. This process, they argue, is explained in part by the internationalisation of political decision-making, the erosion of traditional political cleavages and the changing structure of mass communications. (Poguntke and Webb 2005: 1). Taking the USA as the most obvious example of this sort of arrangement, they conclude that 'modern democracies are moving towards a fusion of elitist and plebiscitary models of democracy, which offer a highly imperfect form of democratic accountability' (*Ibid.*: 142).

Thus the rise of Sarkozy to the position of president of the republic to some extent reflects international trends of depoliticisation. But it also, paradoxically, reflects the more politicised nature of many interest groups and individuals in French society compared with other (in other ways comparable) countries. Ironically, given what I have discussed above in relation to depoliticisation, I have argued that a key to Sarkozy's electoral success was his determination to set about implementing a socio-economic 'modernisation', a reassertion of the values of the right, and a reassertion of the importance of politics as opposed to less ambitious, politico-managerial pragmatism. Sarkozy spoke of the need for a *droite décomplexée*, an unapologetically right-wing right. Part of this was his declared aim to rid France both of its caution and 'political correctness' and its obsession (according to him) with the values born of May 1968. Certainly, there was a degree of vacuousness in all this, but beneath the rhetoric lay a determination to learn from the other modernisers in Western Europe, in particular Margaret Thatcher but also Tony Blair. The similarities between these leaders is highlighted in the preface to the French version of Blair's memoirs, where he encourages Sarkozy to keep pursuing the reform programme. He goes on to say: '[i]f he distances himself from his reforms, he will lose [the 2012 elections]. He was elected in order to bring about change' (Blair 2010).

As far as economic policy is concerned, although Sarkozy's approach has had to change drastically since the onset of the global financial crisis, he has gone out of his way to argue for the right of the private sector to make money and to encourage it to do so. Again, this approach reflects Sarkozy's own career and personal inclinations, which include an unashamed desire to enrich himself and move in moneyed circles. Pierre Musso analyses the agenda and image of the French President in his book *Le Sarkoberlusconisme*, where he contends that there are many similarities between Sarkozy and the Italian Prime Minister Silvio Berlusconi, including the promise to put the country back on its feet via a highly business-oriented economic programme, the heroic new-man image, and a political programme which confronts many supposed enemies, including the foreigner, communism and an over-powerful state (Musso 2008: 26).

In a book which has been much discussed in France, Alain Badiou (2008) places particular emphasis on the authoritarian aspects of Sarkozy's rule and argues that the key to understanding Sarkozy is to compare him with Philippe Pétain; the movement that brought Sarkozy to power has its unconscious roots in Pétainism, which is located between Bonapartism and fascism. In some respects Badiou's thesis is convincing, such as the way he reminds us that there are strong elements of Pétain's rallying cry of *travail, famille, patrie* (work, family, homeland) in Sarkozy's words and deeds, and Badiou suggests the theme of *rupture* is familiar as well, as is the highly law and order-oriented approach to governing, together with the notion of overcoming moral decline and scapegoating particular sections of the population. Pétainism should be understood, Badiou argues, as a phenomenon which pre-dates Pétain himself by many years and which in fact began with the restoration of the monarchy in 1815; in this current the role of negative propaganda as simplification of history and the need for simplistic response is always particularly important: negative propaganda for the restoration concentrated on the decapitation of the king, Pétain's propaganda focused on the Popular Front government of 1936, and Sarkozy's on May 1968. However, although Badiou's analysis is useful in the way in which it identifies certain similarities with the Pétainist right, it underestimates the degree of defeat and/or capitulation of the labour movement and for the mainstream (socialist and communist) left that Pétain's regime reflected. Whereas under Pétain these forces were either driven underground or capitulated, there is today open and active resistance to the Sarkozy reform movement from the left. To an extent, then, it is a case of degree, but degree becomes particularly important in this comparison. Moreover, as others have pointed out, full cooperation with the deportation of tens of thousands of Jews to Germany is, to say the least, a crucial difference between Pétain's regime and Sarkozy's.

Certainly, the mixture of arrogance, autocracy and authoritarianism which plays on the anxieties of ordinary people quickly came to epitomise what has been described as Sarkozy's 'government by fear' (Dakhi et al 2007). It is part of the style, image and conduct which has led various analysts to suggest that he has many of the hallmarks of the archetypal populist leader. This goes to the heart of the (relative) success of the Sarkozy phenomenon and it is perhaps worth dwelling for a moment on the notion of populism. Although the populist label was originally a name given to political groups in late nineteenth-century Russia, in its more extreme forms it has become associated in particular with regimes in Latin America, most notably in Brazil under Getúlio Vargas and in Argentina under Juan Perón, but in many other countries as well in less extreme form. From these examples of populist rule is derived the broader notion which emphasises the importance of the leader's rhetoric, which is intended to encourage support from some of the least progressive (and often underprivileged) sectors of society, a rhetoric which is moralistic, anti-intellectual and lacking in programmatic detail, and which is designed to manipulate and divide. The role of the state (but not parliament) is particularly important, as is loyalty to the leader who becomes a quasi-embodiment of the state, and both voice and protector of the mass of ordinary people (Gellner and Ionescu 1969). These characteristics would certainly seem to apply to Sarkozy's method. An example of his manipulative approach is the way he talks directly to the French people as individuals, but at the same time divides the alleged majority from the minority by suggesting that there are clearly 'good' and 'bad' individuals: those who work hard as opposed to those who do not; those who depend on their own resources and those who constantly expect the state to help them; those who are responsible young people as opposed to *racaille* (rabble); those who are good French citizens as opposed to those who are intruders. It is of course the good ones who are invited to be part of the Sarkozy project and this is also highly reminiscent of Le Pen's populist approach to the mass of ordinary French people.

As far as the future of Sarkozy and Sarkozyism is concerned, two principal questions remain. The first is whether the centre-right is prepared to continue to support Sarkozy as its major representative, despite his unpopularity among the electorate as a whole. The answer to this would seem to be that UMP members and supporters are still, by a large majority, behind the president and are unlikely to switch allegiance to another presidential candidate in the near future. Although Sarkozy's economic and social agenda has

been partially derailed by the economic crisis, it is suffi-
ciently intact that much of the centre-right will continue to
support him. Certainly, there are serious misgivings even
within government over some issues, including the treatment of Roma, for example. But such extreme right-leaning
policies and actions certainly please traditional FN voters
and encourage support from them. The crucial point about
the extreme right is that Sarkozy needs its votes in the second round of the 2012 presidential election, support which
was one of the secrets of his success in 2007.

As I have argued, the success of such a leader also
depends on disarray among opposition forces. The mainstream left opposition to Sarkozy, in the form of the PS, is
certainly in a state of disarray and the PS has arguably been
descending into this situation since the end of the
Mitterrand era in the mid-1990s and perhaps well before
then. Indeed, a politics of left-oriented pragmatism con-
ducted by the PS began in the early to mid-1980s and some
socio-economic 'modernisation' was, paradoxically, con-
ducted under the PS President François Mitterrand
between 1981 and 1995, but this took place via a more consensual type of politics when it seemed France was becoming decreasingly politicised, whereas the trend is now more
complex. The PS has now had three defeats in a row in presidential elections, a record which has provoked further battles over ideological orientation, leadership and strategy.
For example, should the party make a concerted attempt in
the immediate future to open up to the centre? Should it, on
the contrary, return to being a more militant, campaigning
organisation with a stronger orientation towards the labour
movement? Should the party firstly look to other forces
with whom to ally, or get its own house in order before
doing so? In short, the major opposition party is in disarray
and this is of great benefit to Sarkozy. The reassertion of
aggressive politics in this otherwise rather dull landscape,
then, in the form of Sarkozy's unapologetically right-wing
platform, certainly contrasts strikingly with the lacklustre
politics of the PS and open squabbling between its factions,
most of whose stances were variations on the theme of

increasingly centre-oriented positions. The Communist Party, meanwhile, is of course hugely weakened compared with even ten years ago and is not a viable principle party of national government.

The parlous state of the mainstream left has also contributed to the difficulty of constructing a broad-based movement to oppose Sarkozy. Certainly, there have been days of action against particular measures or groups of measures and these have attracted large numbers of participants across France. But there has not been a substantial, effective, ongoing campaign which has either posed a real threat to the reform programme or suggested a viable alternative way forward, although if there had only been very weak resistance there is no doubt that Sarkozy and his government would have gone much further. Beyond the turmoil of the left, we have seen that the reasons for Sarkozy's relative success stem in large part from the approach to change which the regime itself took. First, Sarkozy himself has managed to virtually monopolise media coverage, in part because of his own idiosyncratic behaviour, and thus take the spotlight off opposing forces. Second, the scattergun approach to change — where reforms took place very rapidly and in many different areas simultaneously — meant that any potential opposition was at least partially confused and wrong-footed. Finally, Sarkozy and his colleagues' willingness to negotiate and make concessions over particular measures meant that the wind was often taken out of the sails of those in favour of a different future.

To conclude, I suggest that both the rise of Sarkozy and the nature of his presidential regime is a response to a crisis of hegemony in France. At the beginning of this chapter I made a thumbnail sketch of the various politico-economic stages both France and economically comparable nations have been through since the Second World War. I argued that in France the business community and its allies had at least partially failed to achieve the adjustments they deemed necessary in order for them to compete successfully in a rapidly changing and increasingly global set of economic circumstances. This failure might indeed be

termed a crisis of hegemony, and the maverick and autocratic Sarkozy seemed to have the potential to reconstruct a
type of politico-economic arrangement more acceptable to
the business community while still working within a liberal-democratic framework, albeit with some strain put on
this framework. As we saw in Chapter Two, Gramsci's
notion of hegemony involves the ruling elite taking notice
of and making concessions to some other interests in society, whilst ultimately achieving its own objectives. When
this hegemony breaks down and opposition to these objectives becomes successful in an ongoing way, there is sometimes recourse to a Bonapartist figure in order to attempt to
restore a fuller dominance of the ruling elite. This, I contend,
helps explain both the traditionally-conservative and the
more idiosyncratic—including both left-leaning and
extreme right-leaning—aspects of the Sarkozy phenomenon. The question of how successful this strategy has been
and if it will be successful over the coming years will only be
answered properly in the fullness of time.

Appendices

APPENDIX 1

The French Presidential elections of
22 April and 6 May 2007

First round, 22 April 2007

Total electorate	44,472,834
Voters	37,254,242
Valid votes	36,719,396
Spoilt ballots	1.44%
Abstentions	16.23%

Candidate	Votes	%
Nicolas Sarkozy (Union pour un mouvement populaire)	11,448,663	31.18
Ségolène Royal (Parti socialiste)	9,500,112	25.87
François Bayrou (Union pour la démocratie française)	6,820,119	18.5
Jean-Marie Le Pen (Front national)	3,834,530	10.44
Olivier Besancenot (Ligue communiste révolutionnaire)	1,498,581	4.08

Candidate	Votes	%
Philippe de Villiers (Mouvement pour la France)	818,407	2.23
Marie-Georges Buffet (Parti communiste français)	707,268	1.93
Dominique Voynet (Les Verts)	576,666	1.57
Arlette Laguiller (Lutte ouvrière)	487,857	1.33
José Bové (Alter-mondialiste)	483,008	1.32
Frédéric Nihous (Chasse, pêche, nature, traditions)	420,645	1.15
Gérard Schivardi (Parti des travailleurs)	123,540	0.34

Second round, 6 May 2007

Total electorate	44,472,834
Voters	37,342,004
Valid votes	35,773, 578
Spoilt ballots	4.20%
Abstentions	16.23%

Candidate	Votes	%
Nicolas Sarkozy (Union pour un mouvement populaire)	18,983,138	53.06
Ségolène Royal (Parti socialiste)	16,790,440	46.94

Source: Ministère de l'Intérieur

APPENDIX 2

The French Parliamentary elections of 10 June and 17 June 2007

First round, 10 June 2007

Total electorate	43,896,043
Valid votes	26,521,824
Spoilt ballots	1.13%
Abstentions	39.58%

Second round, 17 June 2007

Total electorate	35,224,832
Valid votes	21,129,554
Spoilt ballots	2.05%
Abstentions	40.03%

Parties and coalitions	1st round, 10 June			2nd round, 17 June			Total seats
	Votes	%	Seats	Votes	%		
Union pour un mouvement populaire	10,289,028	39.54	98	9,463,408	46.37		313
Nouveau centre	616,443	2.37	7	432,921	2.12		22
Divers droite	641 600	2.47	2	238,585	1.17		9
Mouvement pour la France	312 587	1.20	1	-	-		1
Total Presidential Majority	**11,859,658**	**45,58**					**345**
Parti socialiste	6,436,136	24.73	1	8,622,529	42.25		186
Parti communiste français	1 115 719	4.29	0	464,739	2.28		15
Divers gauche	513 457	1.97	0	503,674	2.47		15
Parti radical de gauche	343 580	1.31	0	333,189	1.63		7

Les Verts	845 884	3.25	0	90,975	0.45	4
Total United Left	**9,254,776**	**35,55**				**227**
Mouvement démocrate	1,981,121	7.61	0	100,106	0.49	3
Regionalists	131,585	0.51	0	106,459	0,52	1
Miscellaneous	267,987	1.03	0	33,068	0.16	1
Front national	1 116 005	4.29	0	17,107	0.08	0
Far-left	887 887	3.41	0	-	-	0
Chasse, pêche, nature, tradi-tions	213 448	0.82	0	-	-	0
Other ecologists	208 465	0.80	0	-	-	0
Other far-right	102 100	0.39	0	-	-	0
Total	**26 023 052**	**100**	**110**	**21,130,346**	**100**	**577**

Source: Ministère de l'Intérieur

APPENDIX 3

Abstentions in French presidential elections
(first round only) 1965–2007

Year	% abstentions
1965	15.3
1969	22.4
1974	15.8
1981	18.9
1988	18.6
1995	21.6
2002	28.4
2007	16.2

Source: Ministère de l'Intérieur

APPENDIX 4

Distribution of votes between Sarkozy and Royal according to age and profession.

Second round, Presidential elections, 2007.
% (S= Sarkozy, R=Royal)

Age

18-24 years:	S 42, R 58
25-34 years:	S 57, R 43
35-44 years:	S 50, R 50
45-59 years:	S 45, R 55
60-69 years:	S 61, R 39
70+ years:	S 68, R 32

Profession

Farmers:	S 67, R 33
Craftspeople, shopkeepers:	S 82, R 18
Managerial, liberal professions:	S 52, R 48
Lower supervisory, nurses, primary teachers (*professions intermédiaires*):	S 49, R 51
Clerical:	S 49, R 51
Blue-collar:	S 46, R 54

Source: Ipsos, in *Le Monde* 08.05.07, p. 8.

Le Baromètre de l'action politique - 13 Septembre 2010 - Ipsos / Le Point   APPENDIX 5   Public view of President Sarkozy, 2007-2010.

Le Baromètre de l'action politique - 13 Septembre 2010 - Ipsos / Le Point   APPENDIX 6 *Public view of French Presidents, 1996-2010.*

References and
Bibliography

Algan, Yann and Cahuc, Pierre (2007) *La Société de défiance: comment le modèle social français s'autodétruit.* Paris: Rue d'Ulm.

Ancelovi, Marcos (2008) 'Social Movements and Protest Politics'. In Cole, Alistair, Le Galès, Patrick and Levy, Jonah (eds.) *Developments in French Politics 4.* London: Palgrave, pp. 74–91.

Artufel, Claire and Duroux, Marlène (2006) *Nicolas Sarkozy et la communication.* Paris: Editions Pepper.

Audier, Serge (2008) *La pensée anti-68. Essai sur une restructuration intellectuelle.* Paris: La Découverte.

Badiou, Alain (2008) *Sarkozy. De quoi est-il le nom?* Paris: Lignes.

Badiou, Alain (2009) *The Meaning of Sarkozy.* London: Verso. (trans. by David Fernbach)

Baehr, Peter and Richter, Melvin (eds.) (2004) *Dictatorship in History and Theory: Bonapartism, Caesarism and Totalitarianism.* Cambridge: Cambridge University Press.

Bastien, François (2009) *La constitution Sarkozy.* Paris: Odile Jacob.

Bergounioux, Alain and Werkoff-Leloup, Caroline (2006) *Les Habits neufs de la droite française.* Paris: Plon.

Berstein, Serge (1989) *La France de l'expansion. I. La république gaullienne 1958– 1969.* Paris: Seuil.

Berstein, Serge and Rudelle, Odile (eds) (1992) *Le modèle républicain.* Paris: Presses Universitaires de Paris.

Blair, Tony (2010) *Mémoires.* Paris: Albin Michel.

Braudel, Fernand and Labrousse, Ernest (1982) *Histoire économique et sociale de la France,* vol. 3. *Années 1950 à nos jours.* Paris: Presses Universitaires de Paris.

Brossat, Alain (2007) *Bouffon Impérator.* Paris: Politis.

Cahuc, Pierre and Zylberberg, André (2009) *Les réformes ratées du président Sarkozy.* Paris: Flammarion.

Cannon, Barry (2009) *Hugo Chávez and the Bolivarian Revolution. Populism and Democracy in a Globalised Age.* Manchester: Manchester University Press.

Chafer, Tony and Godin, Emmanuel (eds.) (2010) *The End of the French Exception? Decline and Revival of the 'French Model'*. London: Palgrave.

Choisel, Francis (1987) *Bonapartisme et Gaullisme*. Paris: Albatros.

Chollet, Mona (2008) *Rêves de droite. Défaire l'imaginaire sarkozyste*. Paris: La Découverte.

Cohen, Elie (2008) 'Les trois erreurs de Nicolas Sarkozy'. In *Telos*, 9 May.

Cossé, Pierre-Yves (2010) 'Nicolas Sarkozy et les réformes'. In *Esprit* no. 363, March– April, pp. 58–67. (Special issue entitled *L'Etat de Nicolas Sarkozy*.)

Cowling, Mark and Martin, James (eds) (2002) *Marx's Eighteenth Brumaire. (Post)modern Interpretations*. London: Pluto Press.

Crozier, Michel (1970) *La société bloquée*. Paris: Seuil.

Dagnaud, Monique, 'Qui veut (vraiment) diriger France-Télévisions?' In *Telos* www.telos-eu.com/fr/article/qui_veut_vraiment_diriger_france_televisions (accessed 20 May 2010)

Dakhi, Leyla, Maris, Bernard, Sue, Roger and Vigarello, Georges (2007) *Gouverner par la peur*. Paris: Fayard.

De Gaulle, Charles (1970) *Discours et messages*, vol. 5, *Vers le terme (janvier 1966–avril 1969)*. Paris: Plon.

Dubois, Jean-Pierre (2008a) 'Introduction'. In Ligue des droits de l'homme (ed.) *Une démocratie asphyxiée. L'état des droits de l'homme en France*. Paris: La Découverte, pp. 5–15.

Dubois, Jean-Pierre (2008b), 'Une démocratie asphyxiée'. In Ligue des droits de l'homme (ed.) *Une démocratie asphyxiée. L'état des droits de l'homme en France*. Paris: La Découverte, pp. 17–28.

Duhamel, Olivier (1993) *Le pouvoir politique en France*. Paris: Seuil.

Duhamel, Alain (2009) *La marche consulaire*. Paris: Plon.

Duhamel, Olivier and Field, Michael (2008) *Le Starkozysme*. Paris: Seuil.

Dupin, Eric (2007) *A droite toute*. Fayard: Paris.

Duverger, Maurice (1974) *La monarchie républicaine*. Paris: Robert Laffont.

Faujas, Alain (2007) 'Comment va la France? Dette, chômage, croissance: les réalités d'un pays qui attend son élu(e)'. In *Le Monde*, Dossiers et documents no. 363 (*Comment va la France?*), April, p. 1

Fœssel, Michaël (2010) 'La critique désarmée. L'antisarkozysme qui n'ose pas se dire'. In *Esprit* 363, March–April, pp. 12–13. (Special issue entitled *L'Etat de Nicolas Sarkozy*.)

Forcari, Christophe (2007) 'Le Pen, plus dure est la chute'. In *Libération*, 23 April, p. 9.

Fottorino, Eric (2007) 'Un avertissement adressé à Sarkozy'. In *Le Monde*, 19 June, p. 1.

Fourquet, Jérôme (2007) 'L'échec de Jean-Marie Le Pen à la présidentielle de 2007: les causes d'une hémorragie.'

www.cevipof.msh-paris.fr/bpf/analyses/Fourquet_Le%20pen20
07.pdf (accessed 28 June 2007.)

Fouteau, Carine (2010) 'Immigration: l'état d'expulsion'. In Plenel,
Edwy (ed.) *N'Oubliez pas! Faits et gestes de la présidence Sarkozy.* Paris:
Seuil, pp. 160–6.

Furet, François, Julliard, Jacques and Rosanvallon, Pierre (1988) *La
république du centre.* Paris: Calmann-Levy.

Gamble, Andrew (1994) *The Free Economy and the Strong State. The
Politics of Thatcherism.* 2nd edn. Basingstoke: Macmillan.

Gassama, Makhily (2008) (ed.) *L'Afrique répond à Sarkozy. Contre le
discours de Dakar.* Paris: Philippe Rey.

Gauchet, Marcel and Winock, Michel (2008) 'Une année de
sarkozysme'. In *Le Débat*, 151, September–October, pp. 4–19.

Gellner, Ernst and Ionescu, Ghita (1969) (eds) *Populism: its meaning and
national characteristics.* London: Weidenfeld and Nicolson.

Goodwyn, Lawrence (1978) *The Populist Moment: A Short History of the
Agrarian Revolt in America.* Oxford: Oxford University Press.

Gramsci, Antonio (1971) *Selections from Prison Notebooks.* London:
Lawrence and Wishart.

Grunberg, Gérard and Haegel, Florence (2007) *La France vers le
bipartisme? La Présidentialisation du PS et de l'UMP.* Paris: Presses de
Sciences Po.

Hall, Stuart (2007) *Le populisme autoritaire.* Paris: Editions Amsterdam.

Hall, Ben and Hollinger, Peggy (2009) 'A Pause in Paris'. In *Financial
Times*, 10 November, p. 13.

Hassenteufel, Patrick (2008) 'Welfare Policies and Politics'. In Cole,
Alistair, Le Galès, Patrick and Levy, Jonah (eds) *Developments in
French Politics 4.* London: Palgrave, pp. 209–6.

Hauser, Philippe (2008) 'Forces politiques et ordre policier'. In *Lignes*
25, March.

Hazan, Eric (2007) *Changement de propriétaire. La guerre civile continue.*
Paris: Seuil.

Hermet, Guy (2001) *Les populismes dans le monde. Une histoire
sociologique.* Paris: Fayard.

Hewlett, Nick (1998) *Modern French Politics. Analysing Conflict and
Consensus since 1945.* Cambridge: Polity.

Hewlett, Nick (2003) *Democracy in Modern France.* London and New
York: Continuum.

Hewlett, Nick (2004) 'A Crisis of Democracy?'. In Gaffney, John (ed.)
The French Presidential and Legislative Elections of 2002. Aldershot:
Ashgate, pp. 293–311.

Hewlett, Nick (2007) 'Nicolas Sarkozy and the Legacy of Bonapartism.
The French Presidential and Parliamentary Elections of 2007'. In
Modern and Contemporary France, 15: 4, November, 405–23.

Hewlett, Nick (2010) 'Reviving the French Exception? Sarkozy,
Authoritarian Populism and the Bonapartist Tradition'. In Chafer,
Tony and Godin, Emmanuel (eds) (2010) *The End of the French*

Exception? Decline and Revival of the 'French Model'. London: Palgrave, pp. 39–54.

Hoffmann, Stanley (1967) 'Heroic Leadership: The Case of Modern France'. In Edinger, Lewis J. (ed.) *Political Leadership in Industrialized Societies. Studies in Comparative Analysis*. New York: John Wiley.

Hoang-Ngoc, Liêm (2008) *Sarkonomics*. Paris: Grasset.

Hoang-Ngoc, Liêm (2009) 'La *Sarkonomics* entre promesses électorales et crise économique. Bilan d'étape fin 2008'. In *Modern and Contemporary France* 17: 4, November, 423–34.

Howell, Chris (2008) 'Between State and Market: Crisis and Transformation in French Industrial Relations.' In Cole, A., Le Galès, P. and Levy, J., (eds) *Developments in French Politics 4*. London: Palgrave, pp. 209–26.

Jeanneney, Jean-Marcel (1992) 'L'economie française pendant la présidence du Général de Gaulle'. In Institut Charles de Gaulle (ed.), *De Gaulle en son siècle*, vol. 3, *Moderniser la France*. Paris: La Documentation française/Plon.

Jeudi, Bruno and Vigogne, Ludovic (2007) *Nicolas Sarkozy: de Neuilly à l'Elysée*. Paris: Editions l'Archipel.

Jost, François and Muzet, Denis (2008) *Le téléprésident. Essai sur un pouvoir médiatique*. Paris: Editions de l'aube.

Khiari, Sadri (2009) *La contre-révolution coloniale en France. De de Gaulle à Sarkozy*. Paris: La Fabrique.

King, Anthony (ed.) (2002) *Leaders' Personality and the Outcomes of Democratic Elections*. Oxford: Oxford University Press.

Knapp, Andrew and Sawicki, Frédéric (2008) 'Political Parties and the Party System'. In Cole, Alistair, Le Galès, Patrick and Levy, Jonah (eds) *Developments in French Politics 4*. London: Palgrave, pp. 42–59.

Kuhn, Raymond (2010) '"Les médias, c'est moi." Presidential Media Management in Sarkozy's France.'
http://www.psa.ac.uk/journals/pdf/5/2010/1063_895.pdf (accessed 10 July 2010.)

Laclau, Ernesto (2007) *On Populist Reason*. London: Verso.

Lacorne, Denis (2008) 'Le "rêve américain" du président Sarkozy'. In *Le Débat* 151, September– October, pp. 20–7.

Le Boucher, Eric (2007) 'Entrer dans le siècle'. In *Le Monde*, Dossiers et documents no. 363 (*Comment va la France?*), April, p. 3.

Lecaussin, Nicolas (2008) *L'absolutisme efficace. Enquête sur la présidence de Nicolas Sarkozy*. Paris: Plon.

Leclerc, Henri (2008) 'Sécurité, justice, prisons: éloge de la répression'. In Ligue de droits de l'homme (ed.) *Une démocratie asphyxiée. L'état des droits del'homme en France*. Paris: La Découverte, pp. 5–15.

Lenin, V.I. (1977 [1917]) 'The Beginning of Bonapartism'. In *Lenin Collected Works*. Moscow: Progress Publishers, vol. 25, pp. 223–6.

Lentz, Thierry (1995) *Napoléon III*. Paris: Presses Universitaires de France.

Levy, Jonah (2005) 'Economic Policy and Policy-Making'. In Cole, A., Le Galès, P. and Levy, J. (eds), *Developments in French Politics 3*. Basingstoke: Palgrave, pp. 170–94.

Levy, Jonah, Cole, Alistair and Le Galès, Patrick (2008) 'From Chirac to Sarkozy: A New France?' In Cole, Alistair, Le Galès, Patrick and Levy, Jonah (eds) *Developments in French Politics 4*. London: Palgrave, pp. 1–21.

Leys, Colin (2003) *Market Driven Politics. Neoliberal Democracy and the Public Interest*. London: Verso.

Losurdo, Domenico (2007) *Démocratie ou bonapartisme. Triomphe et décadence du suffrage universel*. Paris: Le Temps des Cerises. (Trans. from Italian by Jean-Michel Goux.)

Magoudi, Ali (2009) *J'vais te dire un truc … Les plus belles déclarations de Nicolas Sarkozy*. Paris: La Découverte.

Maigret, Eric (2008) *L'Hyperprésident*. Paris: Armand Colin.

Marlière, Philippe (2007) 'A gauche, comment combattre le sarkozysme?' In *Mouvements* 52, November–December, pp. 164–69.

Mamère, Noël and Farbiaz, Patrick (2009) *Petits arrangements entre amis. Le Parrain des médias*. Paris: Jean-Claude Gawsewitch.

Marchand, Bernard (1993) *Paris, histoire d'une ville (XIXe– XXe siècle)*. Paris: Seuil.

Marx, Karl (1968) *The Eighteenth Brumaire of Louis Bonaparte*, in Engels, Friedrich and Marx, Karl, *Selected Works*. London: Lawrence and Wishart, pp. 96–179. (First published in 1852.)

MEDEF (2007) *Un besoin d'agir*. Paris: Seuil.

Milza, Pierre (2006) *Napoléon III*. Paris: Editions Perrin.

Mitterrand, François (1962) *Le coup d'état permanent*. Paris: Plon.

Musso, Pierre (2008) *Le Sarkoberlusconisme*. Paris: Editions de l'Aube.

Musso, Pierre (2009) 'Sarkozyisme, néo-télévision et néomanagement'. In *Modern and Contemporary France* 17: 4, 391–406.

Musso, Pierre (2010) 'Le président «télé-réel» d'un etat-entreprise.' In *Esprit* 363, March– April, pp. 33–42. (Special issue entitled *L'Etat de Nicolas Sarkozy*.)

Muxel, Anne (2007) 'La mobilisation électorale. L'envers de 2002 et le sursaut généralisé'. In *Revue française de science politique* 57, pp. 315–28.

Parmentier, Arnaud (2007) 'Le malentendu, déjà?' In *Le Monde*, 19 June, pp. 1–2.

Peloille, Bernard (2009) 'A propos du discours de Nicolas Sarkozy à Bercy, 29 Avril 2007'. In *Cahiers pour l'Analyse Concrète*, pp. 62–3.

Perrineau, Pascal (2008) 'Le Sarkozysme n'est pas une politique de l'instant'. In *Le Figaro*, 9 January, p. 16.

Pinçon, Michel and Pinçon-Charlot, Monique (2010) *Le Président des riches. Enquête sur l'oligarchie dans la France de Nicolas Sarkozy*. Paris: La Découverte.

Plenel, Edwy (2010) 'Le journalisme pris au piège'. In Plenel, E. (ed.) *N'Oubliez pas! Faits et gestes de la présidence Sarkozy*. Paris: Seuil, pp. 86–9.

Plessis, Alain (1985) *The Rise and Fall of the Second Empire, 1852–1871*. Cambridge: Cambridge University Press.

Poguntke, Thomas and Webb, Paul (eds) (2005) *The Presidentialization of Politics*. Oxford: Oxford University Press.

Portelli, Serge (2009) *Le Sarkozysme sans Sarkozy*. Paris: Grasset.

Price, Roger (2002) 'Louis-Napoleon Bonaparte: "Hero" or "Grotesque Mediocrity"?' In Cowling, Mark and Martin, James (eds) *Marx's Eighteenth Brumaire. (Post)modern Interpretations*. London: Pluto Press, pp. 145–62.

Rémond, René (1982) *Les Droites en France*. Paris: Aubier.

Rey, Philippe (ed.)(2008) *L'Afrique répond à Sarkozy: Contre le discours de Dakar*. Paris: Editions Philippe Rey.

Reza, Yasmina (2008) *Dawn, Dusk or Night. A Year with Nicolas Sarkozy*. New York: Knopf.

Ricard, Philippe (2007) 'Une croissance à la traine de l'Europe'. In *Le Monde*, Dossiers et documents no. 363 (*Comment va la France?*), April, p. 3.

Ridet, Philippe (2007) 'L'Elysée. Le péril de l'édredon'. In *Le Monde*, 9 June, pp. 22–3.

Rioux, Jean-Pierre (ed.) (2007) *Les populismes*. Paris: Editions Tempus.

Rozès, Stéphane (2007) 'Epuisement d'un compromis social et contournement politique'. In *La Revue socialiste 29*, October–November.

Sarkozy, Nicolas (2001) *Libre*. Paris: Robert Laffont.

Sarkozy, Nicolas, Collin, Thibaud and Verdin, Philippe (2004) *La république, les religions, l'espérance*. Paris: Pocket.

Sarkozy, Nicolas (2006) *Témoignage*. Paris: XO Editions.

Sarkozy, Nicolas (2007a): *Testimony: France in the Twentieth Century*. New York: Pantheon. (Trans. by Philip H. Gordon.)

Sarkozy, Nicolas (2007b) *Mon Projet. Ensemble, tout devient possible*. Available at www.sarkozy.fr/lafrance/(Accessed 20 February 2008)

Sarkozy, Nicolas (2007c), *Discours à Metz*, 17 April 2007 www.sites.univ-provence.fr/veronis/Discours2007/transcript.php?n=Sarkozy&p=2007-04-17 (Accessed 4 March 2008)

Sarkozy, Nicolas (2007d) *Discours de Bercy*, 29 April 2007 www.sites.univ-provence.fr/veronis/Discours2007/transcript.php?n=Sarkozy&p=2007-04-29 (Accessed 2 February 2009)

Sarkozy, Nicolas (2007e) Speech of Sunday 6 May, Salle Gaveau, Paris, after announcement of election results. Reproduced in full in *Le Monde*, 8 May, pp. 4–5.

Sarkozy, Nicolas (2007f) *Allocation de M. Nicolas Sarkozy, Président de la République, prononcée à l'Université de Dakar, Sénégal, le 23 juillet 2007* www.elysee.fr/elysee/elysee.fr/francais/interventions/2007 (accessed December 2009).

Schwartzenberg, Roger-Gérard (2009) *L'Etat spectacle 2*. Paris: Plon.

Sgard, Jérôme (2007) 'Nicolas Sarkozy, lecteur de Gramsci. La tentation hégémonique du nouveau pouvoir.' In *Esprit*, July.

Sitel, Francis (2010), 'Sous le sarkozysme, la droite ... '. In *Contretemps* 5: 1, 17–26.

Smolar, Piotr (2007) 'Sarkozy place ses hommes à la tête de la police'. In *Le Monde*, 25 May, pp. 1 and 8.

Subileau, Françoise (2001) 'Abstentionnisme'. In Perrineau, Pascal and Reynié, Dominique (eds.) *Dictionnaire du vote*. Paris: PUF, pp. 1–14.

Szarka, Joseph (2009) 'Nicolas Sarkozy as Political Strategist: *Rupture Tranquille* or Policy Continuity?', in *Modern and Contemporary France* 17: 4, 407–22.

Teinturier, Brice (2010) 'Une impopularité historique'. In *Le Nouvel Observateur*, 15–21 July, p. 36.

Tevanian, Pierre (2007) *La république du mépris: les métamorphoses du rascisme dans la France des Années Sarkozy*. Paris: La Découverte.

tns-sofres (2007) 'Les préoccupations des consommateurs-citoyens'. *Vague* 33, mars. www.tns-sofres.com/etudes/pol/28307_preocconso_n.htm (accessed 31 July 2007)

Todd, Emmanuel (2008) *Après la Démocratie*. Paris: Gallimard.

Trotsky, Leon (1940) 'Bonapartism Fascism and War'. www.marxists.org/archive/trotsky/1940/08/last-article.htm (accessed 15 January 2009)

Vassallo, Aude (2005) *La Télévision sous de Gaulle. Le contrôle gouvernemental de l'information, 1958–1969*. Paris: INA-De Boeck.

Vedel, Thierry (2007) *Comment devient-on président/e de la république? Les Stratégies des candidats*. Paris, Laffont.

Volpi, Mauro (1979) *La democrazia autoritaria. Forma di governo bonapartista e V Repubblica francese*. Bologna: il Mulino.

Watkins, Geoff (2002) 'The Appeal of Bonapartism'. In Cowling, Mark and Martin, James (eds) *Marx's Eighteenth Brumaire. (Post)modern Interpretations*. London: Pluto Press, pp. 163–78.

World Economic Forum (2010) 'Cooperation in Labour-Employer Relations', in *Global Competitiveness Report 2010–2011*. Geneva: World Economic Forum.

Zeldin, Theodore (1979) *France 1848–1945. Politics and Anger*. Oxford: Oxford University Press.

Index